A Guide to Her

A GUIDE TO
HERBAL REMEDIES

Mark Evans, MNIMH

Index compiled by
Francesca Garwood-Gowers BA

SAFFRON WALDEN
THE C.W. DANIEL COMPANY LTD

First published in Great Britain by
The C.W. Daniel Company Ltd,
1 Church Path, Saffron Walden,
Essex, CB10 1JP, England.

© Wigmore Publications 1990.

ISBN 0 85207 221 X

This book has been printed on
50% re-cycled paper

Designed by Peter Dolton.
Production in association with Book Production Consultants,
Cambridge, England.
Typeset by J&L Composition Ltd, Filey, North Yorkshire.
Printed in England by
St. Edmundsbury Press, Bury St. Edmunds, England.

Contents

Foreword 7
What is Herbal Medicine? 9
Questions and Answers 15
List of Herbal Medicines in Common Use 19
How to Select and Use Herbal Medicines 21
Symptoms Guide to the Selection of a Medicine 23
Herbal First Aid 49
Herbal Medicines 53
Herbal Medicines for Children's Ailments 71
Veterinary Herbal Medicine 73
Glossary of Terms in Common Use 75
Organisations 79
Suppliers 83
Recommended Reading 85
Index 87

FOREWORD

According to calculations made by the World Health Organisation the use of herbal remedies throughout the world exceeds that of so called conventional drugs by two or three times. This despite the existence since the beginning of this century of a worldwide and influential pharmaceutical industry.

We also know that medicines derived from plants predate any other form of medication and that until the last few centuries all human experience of medicine is based upon them. It is now understood that even animals choose to eat certain plants for 'medical' purposes.

Given this overwhelming dominance it is perhaps surprising that the use of herbs as remedies has such a low profile in English-speaking countries and that a book like this should be necessary. However, following the Industrial Revolution, Britain and the United States (unlike other European cultures) have turned their backs on Nature's remedies and over the last century or so we have lost many of the simple skills of our forbears.

The current return to these skills is thus very welcome; and at the same time considerable scientific evidence has accumulated for the efficacy of herbal remedies. They have their own advantages which complement conventional drugs.

This welcome text lays out very clearly what these advantages are. Mark Evans writes as a leading member of the main professional body of medical herbalists in Britain, with the benefit of personal experience of the use of herbal remedies, supported by a solid scientific background. It serves as a useful introduction to those who would wish to re-acquaint themselves with our original tradition of treatment.

Simon Mills
Joint Director
Centre for Complementary Health Studies
University of Exeter
10th May 1989

What is Herbal Medicine?

Herbal medicine is quite simply the use of plants for healing purposes. As such it lays claim to be the oldest system of medicine in the world since from time immemorial, mankind has used herbs to treat ailments and to promote greater health and well-being. Every culture throughout history has evolved a system of medical treatment using herbs and herbalists today owe a great debt to these centuries of practical experience. The natural world has provided a vast materia medica of medicinal plants; yet we have systematically looked at only a small proportion of the earth's flora.

Origins and Development

From earliest times herbal remedies have been used for treating people. The Egyptians and Greeks acquired considerable knowledge and skill, evolving concepts of health and disease which although superseded by our current knowledge of anatomy, physiology etc still have relevance today. Hippocrates, for example, advocated hygiene, good diet, exercise and herbal medicines as a way of preventing or treating ill-health.

Closer to our own times, medieval herbalists flourished in a resurgence of popular interest in plants and their uses. Practical experience was combined with centuries of classical knowledge by writers such as Nicholas Culpeper, to provide a treasury of information in herbals or early pharmacopaeia. With the expansion of travel, particularly to North America, new ideas and approaches as well as much new herbal medicine enriched and enhanced our native system. It was through such a coming together of English and American trained practitioners that our modern practice has developed;

and in the mid-nineteenth century this amalgamation led to the formation of the National Institute of Medical Herbalists, still the foremost body of professional practitioners in the UK. Modern herbal medicine thus can be seen to have an age-long pedigree deeply rooted in traditional skill and experience but which is increasingly using scientific research to expand and often fully substantiate ancient wisdom.

Principles of Herbal Medicine

The essential nature of herbal medicine is the treatment of people as whole, unique individuals rather than merely a 'cases' of some disease. Although medical herbalists undergo rigorous training to distinguish between symptom patterns when diagnosing illness, they are primarily concerned with establishing the causes of ill-health for each person. Therefore, as well as an assessment of the nature and degree of dysfunction of all the systems in the body, herbalists look at areas such as lifestyle, diet, exercise, stress factors etc in order to gain an overall picture of an individual's health imbalances.

Far from the idea of a 'pill for every ill', herbal medicine can thus involve a good deal of re-education and advice, encouraging people to take greater responsibility for their health and to adopt preventative measures to ensure long-term vitality. This is of course a wider and more positive view of health than the rather restricted aim of symptom relief. Herbal medicine seeks to restore true harmony and wholeness, and it is not surprising, therefore, that one of the commonest phrases a practitioner hears from a patient after treatment is 'I feel so much better in myself'.

Together with advice, the patient will receive individually dispensed herbal medication. There is no such thing as a remedy for an illness, each prescription is unique to the person concerned and subsequent prescriptions may well be altered to adapt to changes in the condition.

The aim of the medicine is to assist the patient's own efforts to regain health. Herein lies another key principle of herbal medicine, the encouragement of the healing processes that are our natural responses to illness. Symptoms are an indication of such responses and are certainly not to be suppressed (except when sometimes they overwhelm our vitality and, even then, only to reduce such excessive reactions).

The medicines used are prepared solely from plant material. In so doing, the medical herbalist rejects the notion of isolating so-called 'active constituents', seeing this as severely disrupting the complex balance of compounds and effects which nature provides. Time and again such isolated constituents and their synthetic 'equivalents', create drug products with little positive effects or dangerous side-effects.

The common drug aspirin well demonstrates this principle. Originally derived from plants rich in salicylate compounds like willow and meadowsweet (after whose Latin name Spiraea the drug was named), aspirin and similar drugs are now well-known to damage the lining of the stomach. Bleeding and even ulceration are not uncommon in long-term use. By contrast, meadowsweet's balance of ingredients enable it to be of great value in gastric problems such as excess acidity and heartburn.

There are many other, similar examples on record which suggest that the very complexity and nature of herbal medicines provide a relatively high degree of safety which in itself is, of course, one of the attractions of this system of healing. The more rounded and often multiple benefits to be derived from plants are a vital part of the herbal approach, quite different from the 'magic bullet' concept which even orthodox medicine has largely discarded.

'Whole plants for whole people' might be a suitable slogan to advertise the principles and practice of Medical Herbalism.

In summary herbal medicine:

1 Treats people rather than diseases, causes rather than symptoms, individuals rather than stereotypes.
2 Uses medication and advice to support the patient's own vital energy and self-healing potential.
3 Prescribes essentially non-toxic herbal treatment derived from the whole plant and not from isolated or synthetic ingredients.

Modern Practice

The importance of the role of the medical herbalist is being re-established in the overall pattern of health care. Recent figures indicate that as many as 1 in 5 people are seeking alternative forms of treatment to conventional medicine, with around 2% of the population having consulted medical herbalists. This represents a resurgence in demand for the herbalist's skills, knowledge and approach to health matters.

Modern herbalists by no means underrate advances in conventional treatment, surgery etc. They would suggest, however, that in many instances such measures are used at too early a stage or to the detriment of general health, and that for many people herbal medicine can provide an alternative, gentler path. Indeed it can often provide answers or possibilities where conventional approaches have none.

Frequently, a visit to the herbalist may be made as a 'last resort' after years of ill-health. It is a powerful testimony that many patients do benefit in this situation, even though treatment can be a lengthy process. From the 1986 'Which' report, patients of medical herbalists reported a remarkable 80% cure or improvement in their condition. Increasingly, many are turning to the individual care and holistic approach of herbal medicine at an earlier stage, and this presents opportunities for preventive measures to be adopted and long-term vitality improved.

It is still the case that education in self-care is an essential part of herbal treatment, and knowledge of the variety of factors involved in illness/health is important in assessing the best plan of action for the individual. For the practitioner today, such an approach is blended with a rigorous training in medical sciences and clinical skills, providing a system of medicine for the present and the future.

Medical herbalists generally practice in a clinic setting, either individually or as part of a group practice. Increasingly, they may operate in a multi-disciplinary clinic, forging links with other therapists whilst establishing a clear role for herbal medicine and respect for its efficacy from professionals and public alike.

In Britain, legal protection for herbalists dates back to the Middle Ages, and in particular to the 'Herbalists Charter' passed by Parliament in Henry VIII's reign to counter excessive restrictive practices on the part of the physicians. Despite a number of attempts to suppress it, herbal medicine has continued through the centuries, thanks to widespread public and Parliamentary support and to the vigilance of practitioners. The National Institute of Medical Herbalists in particular has been at the forefront of ensuring recognition and statutory protection for herbal medicine.

In recent times, and especially within the 1968 Medicines Act, safeguards have been incorporated into legislation regarding the maximum permitted dosage of certain herbs, and/or their restriction of use by qualified practitioners only. At the time of writing, standards of quality and purity of herbal medicines are being raised and this will be valuable in giving greater confidence in the products supplied by manufacturers.

With all these important and necessary changes, it is vital that the unique quality of whole plant extracts be retained and in this respect continuing watchfulness by the public and practitioners is of the greatest importance. The increasing popularity of herbal medicine emphasizes both this need and the necessity of enhanced public protection.

QUESTIONS AND ANSWERS

1 IS HERBAL MEDICINE SAFE?

When prescribed by qualified medical herbalists, the safety record of herbal medicines is impeccable. It is always possible to mis-use any form of medication but herbal medicines are essentially non-toxic and non-addictive, and much safer than synthetic drugs.

2 IS HERBAL MEDICINE EFFECTIVE?

Apart from centuries of traditional use, in itself a testimony to efficacy, very many people in this country and millions world-wide have benefitted from herbal medicine, often after orthodox treatment has failed. A recent survey indicated an 80% improvement or cure rate, which compares very favourably with other therapeutic measures.

Internationally, the medical literature frequently carries positive reports about the efficacy of herbal treatment.

3 IS HERBAL MEDICINE OFFICIALLY RECOGNISED?

Although practitioners are not incorporated in the National Health Service, medical herbalists have long had legal protection and under the Medicines Act of 1968 the profession was granted exemption and the right to practice. The National Institute dates from 1864 and has been granted its own coat of arms.

4 WHERE CAN ONE RECEIVE HERBAL TREATMENT?

There are a number of private practices and clinics throughout the country; addresses and registers for practitioners can be obtained by writing to the professional organisations listed at the back of this book.

5 HOW LONG SHOULD A CONSULTATION LAST?

The first consultation might last an hour or more. This enables the medical herbalist to get a full picture of the patient's health, personal and family medical history (where appropriate) and to provide advice on aspects of lifestyle eg diet, which the patient can use to bring about positive change. The practitioner will then prescribe herbal medicine for that individual. Subsequent consultations involve a reassessment of progress and of the medicine, and are likely to be shorter – around half an hour is typical.

6 WITH WHICH DISEASES CAN HERBAL MEDICINE DEAL?

Herbal medicine is a complete system of treatment and approach to the achievement of health. It aims to encourage and support natural self-healing mechanisms, and by working from the cause of imbalance the patient regains health and so the symptoms disappear. Under qualified treatment, this approach can be of benefit whatever the disease, even if a complete cure cannot be obtained in certain illnesses. It is the person who is treated, rather than the disease.

7 WHERE SHOULD ONE STORE HERBAL MEDICINE?

Herbal medicines should be stored in a cool place, preferably out of direct sunlight. As with all medicines, keep out of the reach of children.

8 HOW LONG CAN THE MEDICINES BE STORED?

Kept correctly, herbal medicines have a long shelf-life but it is better to replace the medicine after a year. Some preparations, such as ointments, last considerably longer; others deteriorate more quickly – follow any instructions carefully.

9 HOW DOES ONE TAKE THE MEDICINES?

When prescribed by a medical herbalist, the directions will be clearly given. For other preparations, follow manufacturers' instructions and also refer to the dosages in this book. Handle as little as possible. In general, the medicines will be taken after meals, unless advised otherwise. REMEMBER, WHEN GIVING HERBAL MEDICINES TO CHILDREN, THE DOSAGE MUST BE REDUCED (see 'How to Select and Use Herbal Medicines' section).

10 WHEN SHOULD ONE STOP TAKING THE MEDICINES?

Again, if consulting a practitioner follow the advice given. Otherwise, if an improvement is noted increase the interval between doses. If the improvement continues, stop taking the medicine; if symptoms worsen again go back to the normal dosage.

11 HOW LONG SHOULD ONE EXPECT TO WAIT BEFORE SEEING A RESULT

With the kind of problems discussed in this book, an improvement in health should be seen within a week. Chronic or more serious conditions, requiring qualified treatment, may of course take a lot longer. If symptoms persist or worsen, consult a qualified medical herbalist or doctor.

12 CAN ONE TAKE HERBAL MEDICINE WITH ORDINARY DRUGS?

Generally the ailments and medicines applicable for self-treatment will present no problems when taken with other drugs. Practitioners will of course take into account any medicines being taken. If in doubt get the advice of the herbalist or doctor.

13 IF SYMPTOMS WORSEN, IS THIS RIGHT?

Herbal medicines stimulate healing responses, and occasionally this can mean an aggravation of the symptoms as the body overcomes the problem. This short-term worsening shows the medicine is working more effectively; if the symptoms get steadily worse without improvement, then change the medicine or get advice.

14 IS IT SAFE TO TAKE HERBAL MEDICINES DURING PREGNANCY?

As a rule it is safer to avoid *any* medication, orthodox or herbal, during pregnancy, unless specifically prescribed by a qualified practitioner. If in doubt seek advice, especially in the first three months of pregnancy.

15 ARE HERBAL MEDICINES SAFE FOR CHILDREN?

Generally, yes. The dosage needs to be adjusted but many can be very helpful for children. It is a good policy to under-dose rather than give too much; for infants seek qualified advice.

16 SOME MEDICINES ARE LABELLED FOR USE IN INDIGESTION, COLDS ETC AS HERBAL MEDICINE IS SAID TO TREAT PEOPLE, ARE THESE ALL RIGHT TO TAKE?

Herbal medicine as a profession does indeed treat people individually. However, many herbal medicines as this book demonstrates, have a wide application in minor complaints and are therefore likely to help large numbers of people. Thousands of people have been introduced to herbal remedies in this way and have achieved successful results. It is still the case that medical herbalists treat the individual and if such general medicines prove ineffective seek advice.

17 IS HERBAL MEDICINE THE SAME AS HOMOEOPATHY?

No. Both systems of treatment seek to establish causes of illness and work on the whole person. Some homoeopathic medicines are derived from herbs but they are prepared and highly diluted in a special way, and the manner of prescribing homoeopathic medicines is quite different. Many homoeopathic remedies are originally from poisonous plants or mineral/animal sources; herbal medicines are from non-toxic herbs only.

18 CAN ANIMALS BE TREATED BY HERBAL MEDICINE?

Yes. Treatment of animals is restricted to qualified vets but there are veterinary herbal medicines available for domestic use. Always remember the size of animals such as dogs or cats is much smaller than people and so the dosages need to be much less.

List of Herbal Medicines in Common Use

The following medicines are some of the most commonly used and most easily obtained. Other medicines not included on this list are available in fewer specialist outlets.

Agrimony
(Agrimonia eupatoria)

Balm
(Melissa officinalis)

Buchu
(Barosma betulina)

Burdock
(Arctium lappa)

Catmint
(Nepeta cataria)

Cayenne
(Capsicum minimum)

Chamomile
(Chamomilla recutita)

Chickweed
(Stellaria media)

Coltsfoot
(Tussilago farfara)

Comfrey
(Symphytum officinale)

Dandelion
(Taraxacum officinale)

Echinacea
(Echinacea angustifolia)

Elderflower
(Sambucus nigra)

Eyebright
(Euphrasia officinalis)

Feverfew
(Tanacetum parthenium or Chrysanthemum parthenium)

Garlic
(Allium Sativa)

Ginger
(Zingiber officinale)

Horehound
(Marrubium vulgare)

Hyssop
(Hyssopus officinalis)

Lavender
(Lavandula officinalis)

Lime Blossom
(Tilia europaea)

Marigold
(Calendula officinalis)

Marshmallow
(Althaea officinalis)

Meadowsweet
(Filipendula ulmaria)

Nettle
(Urtica dioica)

Oats
(Avena sativa)

Peppermint
(Mentha piperita)

Raspberry Leaf
(Rubus idaeus)

Red Clover
(Trifolium pratense)

Rosemary
(Rosmarinus officinalis)

Sage
(Salvia officinalis)

Slippery Elm
(Ulmus fulva)

Thyme
(Thymus vulgaris)

Valerian
(Valeriana officinalis)

Witch Hazel
(Hamamelis virginiana)

Yarrow
(Achillea millefolium)

The following preparations are also included in the book:

Tincture of Myrhh
Comfrey Ointment
Calendula Ointment
Essential Oil of Lavender
Essential Oil of Rosemary
Essential Oil of Tea Tree
Black Horehound
(Ballota Nigra)

How to Select and use Herbal Medicines

This guide relates to common minor ailments which can usually be treated at home. However, chronic or serious conditions require treatment by a qualified practitioner – if in doubt, seek advice and help in this way.

1 Note your main symptoms and, if possible, the immediate causes.

2 Study the SYMPTOMS GUIDE to find a selection of herbal medicines which may be appropriate.

3 Study the HERBAL MEDICINES section carefully to gain more information on the suggested herbs and to find the dosage – REMEMBER this is normally repeated three times a day.

4 You do not have to experience all symptoms listed under a medicine; the properties described and the areas of use will help you to decide if it is suitable for you.

5 Methods of taking herbal medicines:

a) Tablets – compare strength of tablet with recommended dosage in the HERBAL MEDICINES section, and take the number required to equal this.

b) Other standardised preparations such as tinctures, syrups etc, follow the manufacturers instructions.

c) For home preparations from the herbs themselves, see table below:

Part of plant:	Leaf and/or flower	Root or bark
Preparation most suitable:	Infusion	Decoction
Method used:	Pour 500ml boiling water onto 25g herb(s). Cover. Leave for 10 minutes. Strain.	Simmer 25g herb(s) in 500ml of water for 10 minutes Strain.
Dosage:	20ml of infusion is equivalent to 1g of herb. Find recommended dosage in HERBAL MEDICINES section.	20ml of decoction is equilavent to 1g of herb. Find recommended dosage in HERBAL MEDICINE section.

These home preparations need to be refrigerated and will only last 3–4 days.

Note 1 gram (g) = 1,000 milligrams (mg)
    28g = 1 ounce
    1 litre = 1,000 millilitres (ml)
    450ml = 1 pint
    5ml = 1 teaspoon
    20ml = 1 tablespoon

d) All the dosages recommended in this book are appropriate for adults. Frail, elderly people will usually respond to half these dosages. For children, dosages MUST be reduced as follows:–

Age 11–14 ¾ recommended dosages.

Age 7–10 ½ recommended dosages.

Age 4–6 ¼ recommended dosages.

Age under 4 years, generally seek advice first.

Symptoms Guide to the Selection of a Medicine

The approach of herbal medicine entails seeking the causes of ill-health rather than simply treating the symptoms; this guide is for self-treatment of minor ailments in the home. IF SYMPTOMS ARE SERIOUS, UNEXPLAINED OR PROLONGED, CONSULT A MEDICAL HERBALIST OR A DOCTOR.

To select an appropriate medicine, consult the symptoms guide to find the problem and medicines most suitable for it. For more information on each medicine listed and dosage levels, refer to the Herbal Medicines section. The medicines under each symptom are listed alphabetically NOT in order of priority, although many other medicines not covered by this book may be used by medical herbalists, those listed are a selection of the most widely available and suitable for domestic use.

Abscess

A localised inflamed swelling containing pus. Apart from those developing on the skin, abscesses can develop internally and should be referred for treatment.

Treatment See BOIL

Acne

Widespread inflamed spots most often found during puberty and related partly to the hormonal changes at this time and partly due to dietary intolerances. Restricting sweet, fatty and refined foods and eating plenty of fresh fruit and vegetables is nearly always helpful.

Treatment See Boil

Anxiety

Tension and chronic stress are becoming more common, and treatment may need to focus on many areas of life. Prolonged or high levels of anxiety required qualified help. See also NERVOUS PROBLEMS.

Treatment Balm, Chamomile, Lavender, Lime Blossom, Oats, Valerian

> **Balm** can be taken over a period of time for mild anxiety, with or without depression.

> **Chamomile** Gently relaxing, especially useful where nervous indigestion accompanies anxiety.

> **Lavender** For irritability, tension headaches and effects of chronic stress.

> **Lime Blossom** Helpful in restoring normal sleep after nervous disturbances, also calms the stomach and eases nervous palpitations.

> **Oats** The best remedy for nervous exhaustion and debility, gradually restoring nerve function to normality.

> **Valerian** Strongly relaxant but without being a depressant. For acute anxiety and tension.

Athletes Foot

A fungal skin condition, often with considerable itching and irritation. Usually occurs between the toes but can be found elsewhere, for example in the groin. It is important to keep the affected area as cool and dry as possible, to discourage fungal spread. If infection persists or recurs, seek qualified advice.

Treatment Marigold, Myrrh, Tea Tree

> **Marigold** and also **Tincture of Myrrh**, are both extremely useful when applied locally to combat the fungal growth. The application should be left to dry on the skin. This can be backed up by the use of foot baths with 10 drops of essential oil of **Tea Tree** added – dry feet carefully after foot-bath.

Boil

Localised inflammation on the skin, with pus-filled swelling. A multi-headed and deeper seated area is termed a carbuncle.

Treatment Burdock, Echinacea, Marshmallow, Red Clover, Slippery Elm

> **Burdock** Powerful cleanser for the tissues in general, where high level of toxins need to be removed.
>
> **Echinacea** Another cleansing alternative, especially useful to increase resistance to infection and to improve circulation to the skin.
>
> **Marshmallow** Used externally as a hot poultice from the powdered leaf, particularly when combined with powdered **Slippery Elm**, sooths the inflamed area and encourages the spot to draw to a head and discharge the pus.
>
> **Red Clover** Gentle but very effective alternative, clearing inflamed spots, acne etc. It can also be used externally to bathe the area, mild enough for use on children.

Bronchitis

Acute inflammation of the membranes lining the airways which lead into the lungs. Can often recur, especially in the elderly, and is a source of chronic ill-health. Bronchitis with chest pains which gets worse with painful coughing should be referred for qualified treatment, as should any chronic condition.

Treatment Cayenne, Coltsfoot, Comfrey, Garlic, Ginger, Horehound, Hyssop, Marshmallow, Thyme

> **Cayenne** And to a lesser extent **Ginger**, stimulates the circulation and induces warmth when Bronchitis is made worse by cold, damp weather.
>
> **Coltsfoot** Excellent to ease dry, spasmodic coughing with little or no mucus.
>
> **Comfrey** For a painful cough with a tight feeling across the chest.

Garlic Increases ability to fight and resist infection, and stimulates the removal of excess mucus. Particularly effective when used raw.

Horehound For congestion in the lungs with thick, sticky mucus which is not easily removed by coughing.

Hyssop Dry cough with irritation; gently releases the tension which often accompanies bronchial spasm. Particularly good for children.

Marshmallow Highly soothing, use whenever the membranes are inflamed and coughing is painful.

Thyme Expectorant and anti-infective, loosening mucus and relieving bronchial congestion.

Bruises   See FIRST AID SECTION

Burns   See FIRST AID SECTION

Carbuncle   See BOIL

Catarrh

Over-production of mucus in the respiratory system. If occurring lower down this produces bronchial catarrh and congestion (see BRONCHITIS). Upper respiratory catarrh can often follow recurrent colds (see COMMON COLD). If catarrh is prolonged or severe, seek qualified treatment to determine the causes.

Treatment Agrimony, Catmint, Elderflower, Eyebright, Hyssop, Peppermint

Agrimony Helps to astringe and tone the congested mucus membranes and reduce excessive catarrhal discharge.

Catmint Improves the circulation, eases nasal congestion and catarrh.

Elderflower For sinusitis with blocked passages and thick mucus.

Eyebright To relieve watery nasal discharge, with puffiness under the eyes.

Hyssop Stuffed-up nose with thick, sticky phlegm, useful if sleep affected by congestion, as it is also a gentle relaxant.

Peppermint For severe congestion use in the short-term only, as an inhalation – drops of the essential oil can be added to steaming water.

Chilblains

Red, itchy swellings on the fingers or toes due to insufficient circulation. This leads to the blood vessels of the extremities going into spasm with changes in temperature; layers of clothing, which trap air between them, are a useful precaution.

Treatment Cayenne, Ginger, Lime Blossom, Yarrow

Cayenne and **Ginger** strongly stimulate the circulation.

Lime Blossom and **Yarrow** are more gentle, acting to dilate the blood vessels.

Colic

Bouts of spasmodic cramping pains, usually associated with gas and/or excessive tension in the bowel wall (see also DYSPEPSIA and FLATULENCE). It can, however, be due to more serious imbalances; if persistent seek the guidance of a qualified doctor.

Treatment Catmint, Chamomile, Ginger, Lavender, Valerian

Catmint Flatulence and indigestion/colic linked to anxiety and tension. Gentle and useful in a variety of digestive upsets.

Chamomile For all minor digestive problems related to tension or over-eating. Excellent for children's colic.

Ginger Warming anti-spasmodic, very effective in relieving colic which is aggravated by cold.

Lavender Relaxes muscles of the bowel walls; for nervous irritability with excess tension – also helpful to improve digestion following mild depression; is balancing in action.

Valerian Short-term acute tension induced colicky spasms.

Common Cold

Viral infection of the upper respiratory system. If this recurs frequently, attention needs to be focussed sharply upon improving resistance. In this respect, medical herbalists can offer considerable help on an individual basis and their advice should be sought.

Treatment **Elderflower, Ginger, Peppermint, Yarrow**

> Once contracted, there is no magical herbal cure for colds but the above remedies will do a great deal to improve circulation and relieve nasal congestion (see also CATARRH). The simplest method is to make a tea with 1 teaspoon of each herb and drink hot, sipping frequently.

Conjunctivitis

Inflammation of the membrane covering the front surface of the eye. This can be a result of cold draughts, a local irritant in the eye or an infection. Generally eye conditions are not to be treated at home other than for the simplest problems, so do not delay seeking medical advice.

Treatment **Chamomile, Eyebright, Marigold**

> All these medicines have anti-inflammatory properties and may be used as a local compress, from a cooled infusion, as a short-term aid only.

Constipation

Reduced frequency of bowel movement, often with difficulty and pain and hard stools. Straining to empty the bowels can lead to bleeding from haemorrhoids (see HAEMORRHOIDS). Constipation can frequently result from insufficient dietary fibre, lack of exercise especially of the abdominal muscles and shallow breathing which under-uses the diaphragm, and/or posture. However, bowel muscles can also become over-tensed due to stress and anxiety, and this situation should not be treated with any laxative medicine or concentrated fibre like bran. Get qualified treatment for individual correction.

Treatment Burdock, Chamomile, Dandelion, Valerian

>**Burdock** Gently stimulating bowels, useful where sluggishness accompanies an accumulation of poisons in the system eg in skin problems such as acne.
>
>**Chamomile** Over-tense bowels and poor digestion, with liverish sensation.
>
>**Dandelion** One of the best, gentle laxatives, improving muscle tone and bowel movement without causing griping.
>
>**Valerian** Stress-induced bowel spasm and constipation.

Convalescence

The period of recovery from illness often neglected but very important, in particular for chronic or debilitating illnesses such as glandular fever. The convalescent stage of most ailments can feature symptoms such as lack of appetite, poor digestion, depreison and fatigue or exhaustion. Alongside rest and simple, nourishing foods, herbal medicines can help to restore normal energy levels.

Treatment Balm, Oats, Rosemary, Slippery Elm

>**Balm** Lack of appetite and poor digestive action, following illness or chronic stress. Can be taken for prolonged periods.
>
>**Oats** Nervous exhaustion and debility, with mild depression and lack of energy which slows down recovery.
>
>**Rosemary** Feelings of apathy and no energy, often with sluggish digestion and/or muzzy headaches.
>
>**Slippery Elm** Use as a dietary supplement during convalescence when appetite is poor and there is difficulty in digesting foods.

Coughs

A reaction to any irritation or inflammation in the airways. Like most symptoms, the cough reflex can have vital importance; in this case by keeping the bronchial tubes open, and it should not normally be suppressed but help given to make coughing more effective and productive (see also BRONCHITIS)

Treatment Coltsfoot, Comfrey, Horehound, Hyssop, Marshmallow, Thyme

> **Coltsfoot** To loosen and calm a dry, spasmodic cough with irritation in the airways.
>
> **Comfrey** Very soothing, useful for harsh, painful coughing with tight feeling in chest.
>
> **Horehound** Excellent expectorant to loosen a cough where there is a little production of a thick and sticky mucus.
>
> **Hyssop** For nervous, irritating cough; sooths locally and generally calms tension and restlessness.
>
> **Marshmallow** A relaxant, highly soothing expectorant, where the passages are inflamed and coughing is painful.
>
> **Thyme** To relieve a dry cough with bouts of spasmodic wheezing and coughing.

Cuts, Grazes etc   See FIRST AID SECTION

Cystitis

Inflammation of the lining of the bladder, causing painful urination with irritation in the bladder region and frequent urging to pass water. Experienced more by women and often a recurrent problem which may be associated with vaginal infections or possibly small gravelly deposits in the urinary system. If persistent or recurrent see a qualified medical herbalist. In the short-term, single measures include taking plenty of fluid (but not alcohol) and resting, especially with some warmth such as a hot-water bottle to relax the muscles.

Treatment Agrimony, Buchu, Chamomile, Echinacea, Garlic, Marshmallow, Meadowsweet, Yarrow

> **Agrimony, Meadowsweet, Yarrow** These medicines have astringent properties, toning up the inflamed membranes and increasing the flow of urine.
>
> **Buchu** For relieving painful, burning sensations on passing urine.

Chamomile Eases inflammation and relaxes over-taut bladder muscles which can slow down urination.

Echinacea Garlic These medicines strongly stimulate resistance to infection; to be taken for some time after acute symptoms have subsided, in order thoroughly to cleanse the tissues.

Marshmallow Very soothing, can be taken when there is pain or discomfort with passing urine.

Debility & Depression See NERVOUS PROBLEMS

Diarrhoea

Looseness and frequency of bowel movements. As a short term reaction to infection, food poisoning or inflammation, diarrhoea can be a helpful, cleansing action – but severe or prolonged loose motions represent a serious imbalance needing urgent qualified treatment. Take plenty of fluids to replace that lost in bowel movements.

Treatment Agrimony, Catmint, Chamomile, Garlic, Meadowsweet, Slippery Elm, Thyme, Witch Hazel

Agrimony Useful in mild gastroenteritis and other upsets with diarrhoea.

Catmint For nervous diarrhoea eg from pre-exam nerves. Mild enough for children.

Chamomile Generally soothing and anti-inflammatory for the digestion tract, especially where looseness is due to worry or over-eating. Excellent for children's minor upsets.

Garlic To resist gastric infections, even mild food poisoning.

Meadowsweet Acid indigestion, especially if accompanied by diarrhoea.

Slippery Elm Soothing to inflamed tract, particularly valuable as a food supplement for elderly people with occasional diarrhoea.

Thyme Digestive infections with churning sensation and loose bowels.

Witch Hazel Astringent action on irritated, inflamed bowels; good where diarrhoea is linked with haemorrhoids.

Dyspepsia

Indigestion, which may be accompanied by bloating and gas, heartburn or other digestive pains, nausea or even vomiting and/or bowel disturbances. (See also CONSTIPATION, DIARRHOEA, FLATULENCE and NAUSEA). Initial steps including checking the diet and how quickly or thoroughly foods are chewed; the amounts of food in a meal and the degree of stress at mealtimes – for most families with children look no further! Persistent gastric/digestive pain will, as always need qualified treatment. Often combinations of herbal medicines, to suit the individual, are needed depending on the causes of the indigestion.

Treatment Agrimony, Balm, Chamomile, Dandelion, Meadowsweet, Peppermint, Slippery Elm

> **Agrimony** For acid indigestion and gastric discomfort, especially if bowels are loose.
>
> **Balm** Nervous indigestion, with churning sensations and flatulence.
>
> **Chamomile** Gently balancing digestive system; for the effects of anxiety and over-rich foods, such as stomach pains and inflammation, excessive gas, nausea etc.
>
> **Dandelion** For discomfort from poor, sluggish digestion, with mild biliousness and constipation.
>
> **Meadowsweet** Relieves heartburn and acid dyspepsia.
>
> **Peppermint** Flatulent indigestion, giving spasmodic bloating pains; also useful for chills which affect the stomach.
>
> **Slippery Elm** Painful dyspepsia arising from some inflammation – will soothe and tone the affected membranes.

Earache

If all prolonged or increasing in severity, seek medical advice.

Eye Problems

Apart from the simplest conditions, eye problems should be referred for qualified treatment. Inflammation of the eyelids or of the conjunctiva may in the short-term be helped by eye pads or eyebaths.

Treatment See CONJUNCTIVITIS

Fever

The response of the body to a raised body temperature, usually associated with an infection. The range of diseases which can provoke the fever response vary from colds and influenza, where home treatment can be very helpful, to serious, even life-threatening, conditions. If unsure of the problem or if fever persists SEEK QUALIFIED ADVICE. The procedure is to take the temperature and assess the feelings of cold/warmth; the fever is essentially a healthy response to trouble. At body temperatures of 100–101° beneficial events may be occuring. (38°C). See also COMMON COLD and INFLUENZA.

Treatment Catmint, Elderflower, Garlic, Hyssop, Lime Blossom, Peppermint, Yarrow

> **Catmint, Elderflower, Peppermint, Yarrow** These medicines are all diaphoretic, that is inducing perspiration and improving the distribution of heat throughout the body. They act to normalise temperatures, especially when the person is hot and restless with little or no sweating.
>
> **Garlic** Warming anti-infection, especially useful for chills or shivering in the early phase of infections.
>
> **Hyssop, Lime Blossom** Diaphoretic, with additional relaxant effect to calm the irritability which often accompanies a feverish condition.

Flatulence

The production of excessive gas in the digestive tract, causing discomfort, bloating and pains. Can be due to a variety of problems. If prolonged get qualified herbal treatment. See also COLIC and DYSPEPSIA.

Treatment Balm, Catmint, Cayenne, Chamomile, Ginger, Peppermint, Rosemary, Thyme

> **Balm** Anxiety-related flatulence, stemming from tension and/or depression.
>
> **Catmint** Spasmodic pains and bloating from mild nervousness.
>
> **Cayenne** Highly warming, valuable where a poor digestion and feelings of cold lead to colic or flatulence. NOT for acute stomach inflammation or heartburn.
>
> **Chamomile** Generally soothing carminative, useful both where gas due to tension or effects of over-eating.
>
> **Ginger** Somewhat more gently warming than **Cayenne**, particularly good for relieving gas and spasms in the bowels.
>
> **Peppermint** To relieve flatulence and bloating from irritability, tension or biliousness – relaxing to over-stretched walls of the intestinal tract.
>
> **Rosemary** For wind from depression and sluggish liver/digestive activity.
>
> **Thyme** Improving digestion especially helpful where there is too much fat in the diet, with bloating and feeling of fullness.

Gastritis See Dyspepsia

Haemorrhoids

Swollen veins in the rectal passage, occasionally protruding externally or bleeding with bowel movements. Often associated with chronic constipation and constant straining to empty the bowels. Improvements in diet, with a wide variety of wholefoods to increase dietary fibre, combined with exercises can often work wonders. For individual treatment see a medical herbalist.

Treatment Comfrey, Marigold, Witch Hazel

>Any of these remedies used externally, as an ointment, paste or lotion, will help to astringe and tone the swollen, inflamed tissues.

Hayfever (Allergic Rhinitis)

Allergic reaction to a varying number of grass, flower and/or tree pollens, with violent bouts of sneezing and inflammation of the nasal passages. Often the eyes are affected, leading to burning or smarting sensations and profuse weeping. For medical herbalists, hayfever is seen as part of a wider sensitivity, often showing up with asthma or eczema and commonly appearing in families through the generations. Additionally allergies to, for example, different foods can contribute to the problem. Therefore, seek qualified treatment.

Treatment Chamomile, Eyebright

>**Chamomile** Used locally as an eye pad (soaked in a cooled infusion) to relieve inflammation around the eyes. Also internally to ease the nasal congestion and calm the irritated membranes.

>**Eyebright** Use externally as above and internally to reduce the copious, watery catarrh and explosive sneezing.

Headache

Can develop from a number of causes, most commonly anxiety and tension, nasal congestion from colds or sinusitis, muscle spasm or digestive upsets such as biliousness or constipation. Other conditions which may produce headaches, for instance high blood pressure, obviously require qualified treatment. If in doubt get help. See also MIGRAINE.

Treatment Chamomile, Lavender, Lime Blossom, Peppermint, Rosemary

>**Chamomile** Dull, throbbing headache with irritability. Also stemming from indigestion and bilious sensations, perhaps from over-eating rich foods.

Lavender Tension headaches. Also useful externally; rub the essential oil (1–2 drops only) gently into the temples to relieve pain.

Lime Blossom Pains from anxiety and stress, especially if used at an early stage, and where headaches are eased by applying local warmth.

Peppermint Spasmodic pains with a 'hot head', and for indigestion related headaches.

Rosemary Headache related to tension or depression and sluggish liver (eg hangovers, use with **Chamomile** or **Peppermint**). Helps to reduce blood vessels spasm.

Heartburn   See Dyspepsia

Indigestion   See Dyspepsia

Influenza

Viral infection of the respiratory system, producing feverishness and aching muscles, often accompanied by coughing, headache and a general feeling of weakness. In elderly people it can be seriously debilitating. See also COMMON COLD and FEVER.

Treatment Catmint, Cayenne, Echinacea, Elderflower, Garlic, Ginger, Hyssop

Catmint Congestion in the nose and throat with local heat. Gently calms associated restlessness and irritability.

Cayenne Improves circulation and warmth in the early stages of 'flu, where there are feelings of chill or cold.

Echinacea For weakness or debility and poor resistance to infections, with feeling of cold.

Elderflower Feverish symptoms, with nasal congestion – aids sweating and regulates temperature.

Garlic Helps fight infections and ward off any complications such as bronchitis.

Ginger Similar to **Cayenne**, not so fiercely stimulating to the circulation. Induces a cleansing sweat.

Hyssop Good for children, or adults, unable to sleep during influenza symptoms because of restlessness and agitation.

Insomnia

Sleeplessness, due to a variety of causes, notably anxiety or worry. It is very important to tackle these factors and not become dependent on sedatives. Use mildly relaxing herbal medicines to aid a return to natural sleep patterns; if insomnia persists get professional advice. See also ANXIETY and NERVOUS PROBLEMS.

Treatment Balm, Chamomile, Hyssop, Lavender, Lime Blossom, Valerian

Balm Helps to restore balance to the nervous system; mild enough to use for children.

Chamomile Gentle relaxant, especially useful where nervous indigestion disturbs sleep.

Hyssop Insomnia related to worry and restlessness, especially associated with nasal congestion or 'flu.

Lavender Nervous tension and even exhaustion, leading to inability to have refreshing sleep

Lime Blossom For tension-related insomnia and mild headaches.

Valerian Strongly relaxant, but without producing the depression associated with sleeping pills. Use as short-term aid for acute stress-linked insomnia.

Itching See SKIN PROBLEMS

Laryngitis

Inflammation of the vocal chords, producing hoarseness or even loss of voice. Often accompanied by **CATARRH**.

Treatment **Agrimony, Echinacea, Marshmallow, Raspberry Leaf, Sage, Thyme**

> **Agrimony, Raspberry Leaf, Sage, Thyme** All have mildly astringent properties and can be used as gargles, especially in tincture form, to tone up the throat.
>
> **Echinacea** General stimulant to the immune system, improving resistance to infections, catarrh etc.
>
> **Marshmallow** Soothing anti-inflammatory remedy, acting through the reflexes to calm the pain and irritation and improve catarrhal state.

Menopause

When menstrual cycle ceases; often called the change of life. The priority for medical herbalists is to help the body adjust to the hormonal and other changes taking place rather than delay the process with hormone replacement. If there are difficulties then seek qualified treatment.

Treatment **Chamomile, Oats**

> **Chamomile** To relieve nervous irritability and/or fluid retention which often occur during menopausal changes.
>
> **Oats** Tiredness and exhaustion, a feeling of slowing down with a lack of energy.

Menstrual Disorders   See PERIOD PAINS

Migraine

Severe headache, often localised over one eye, and may be accompanied by disturbed vision, flashing lights or similar symptoms Nausea and even vomiting can occur. A complex problem, usually needing professional attention to establish the cause(s). See also HEADACHE.

Treatment **Chamomile, Feverfew, Rosemary, Valerian**

> **Chamomile** Dull, throbbing ache, perhaps with some nausea or biliousness
>
> **Feverfew** Feeling of having a tight band around the head, pains relieved by local warmth.

Rosemary Good for headaches brought on by tension/depression; can also be used when local warm application gives relief.

Valerian For anxiety and tension-related Migraines.

Morning Sickness

Feelings of nausea or actual vomiting during the first three months of pregnancy. It can occur throughout the day, despite its name, and low blood sugar levels are an important causative factor.

Treatment Chamomile, Ginger, Meadowsweet, Peppermint

All these medicines may give relief from the nausea and settle the stomach. Probably the best method is a weak infusion sipped frequently, perhaps with the addition of a little honey.

Mouth Ulcers

Small but painful ulcers found on the tongue, gums or lining of the mouth. Can break out in numbers and are often a sign of general debility – this indicates a need to improve general health as well as local treatment.

Treatment Marigold, Myrrh, Sage, Thyme

These remedies, particularly in tincture form, are highly effective used locally as mouthwashes or gargles, astringing the tissues and stimulating healing.

Muscular Aches & Pains

Can be due to a variety of causes, notably over-exercise or strain of the muscles, or rheumatic inflammation (see also RHEUMATIC PROBLEMS). A combination of rest and gentle exercise is likely to help.

Treatment Lavender, Rosemary

External use of the essential oils of these two herbs (see under **LAVENDER** for directions) can be of great value in relieving muscle spasm and inflammation.

Nausea

Feelings of nausea can arise in many situations, from over-eating and drinking to motion sickness or wider illnesses. If persistent or unexplained get help. For treatment to relieve symptoms apply the remedies for MORNING SICKNESS.

Nervous Problems

Increasingly, our nervous systems are being affected by environmental factors, lifestyle and long-term stress, leading to nervous exhaustion and debility. Obviously, serious disorders such as schizophrenia, psychosis etc need medical attention but early attention to signs of stress can pay tremendous dividends. See also ANXIETY.

Treatment Lavender, Lime Blossom, Rosemary, Oats, Valerian

> **Lavender** Tension and irritability, perhaps leading to mild depression. May also experience colicky pains or tension headaches.
>
> **Lime Blossom** Mild but persistent anxiety or nervousness, perhaps linked with palpitations during stress.
>
> **Rosemary** Nervous exhaustion and depression, irritability from fatigue.
>
> **Oats** Generally run-down, tired and lacking in energy, especially from chronic stress or a long illness.
>
> **Valerian** General nervous and muscular tension; especially when involving insomnia as a short-term relief or to help wean off sedative drugs.

Period Problems

Menstrual disorders can be of various kinds, with painful, heavy, irregular or very light periods, pre-menstrual tension and bloating etc. Any Persistent problems will require qualified treatment. Also see Menopause.

Treatment Balm, Chamomile, Peppermint, Valerian

> **Balm** Gentle relaxant, can be safely taken over a long time for premenstrual tension or painful periods.
>
> **Chamomile** Anti-inflammatory, anti-spasmodic effect, of value throughout the menstrual cycle where muscle spasms or tension cause problems.
>
> **Peppermint** Particularly useful for relieving period pains accompanied by feelings of nausea.
>
> **Valerian** Relieves cramping, spasmodic pains during menstruation and calms excess irritability.

Piles   See HAEMORRHOIDS

Poor Circulation

Insufficient blood supply to the extremities, with very cold hands or feet, is fairly common – especially among the elderly. The condition is aggravated by smoking, amongst other factors, and can lead to serious disease.

Treatment Cayenne, Elderflower, Garlic, Ginger, Hyssop, Lime Blossom, Nettle, Rosemary, Yarrow

> Most of these remedies work to dilate the blood vessels at the extremities, and so help to improve circulation – see under each herb in the MEDICINES SECTION for other properties. *Ginger* and most notably, **Cayenne**, act more positively to stimulate blood flow through the tissues.

Pregnancy

A variety of problems can arise during pregnancy; regular ante-natal check-ups are important to monitor health. If in doubt get medical advice. Also see MORNING SICKNESS.

Treatment Raspberry Leaf

> **Raspberry Leaf** Helps to relax pelvic muscles in preparation for labour, improving the efficiency of uterine contractions in labour.

Rheumatism

Inflammation either of muscles or tissues around the joints. Needs complex qualified herbal treatment to establish underlying imbalances and work individually. Often an improvement in elimination is required, especially via the kidneys.

Treatment Dandelion, Ginger, Lavender, Meadowsweet, Nettle

> **Dandelion** Cleansing waste matter from the tissues and stimulating the liver (root preparations) or kidneys (leaf preparations).
>
> **Ginger** For stiffness and aches made worse by cold, damp weather – improves circulation through muscles.
>
> **Lavender** Externally very valuable to relax and warm tight, painful muscles and joints.
>
> **Meadowsweet** Relieves pain and inflammation, also increasing elimination through the kidneys.
>
> **Nettle** Where circulation is poor; acts as blood cleanser, providing minerals essential for tissue repair and renewal.

Scalds   See FIRST AID SECTION

Sciatica

Pain and inflammation of the sciatic nerve which extends from the lower back through the pelvis and down the legs. Often due to a structural problem in the spine and/or pelvis. Manipulation may be required.

Treatment Chamomile, Lavender, Valerian

> **Chamomile** For dull aching sensation in thighs and back of legs, with slight inflammation.
>
> **Lavender** Essential Oil used externally in dilution, to relax muscles of the area and provide local warmth.
>
> **Valerian** Sharper pains, with cramping spasms in the thigh or leg.

Shingles

Painful clusters of blisters at nerve endings, caused by the same virus that produces chickenpox. Often seen in the elderly and is usually a sign of debility.

Treatment Lavender, Oats, Rosemary

> In their own way, each of these medicines act as tonics for the nervous system, helping to rebuild vitality. For mild outbreaks of shingles, the external use of essential oil of **Lavender** may be helpful to relieve the persistent pain.

Sinusitis

Inflammation of the sinus cavities, often accompanied by catarrh and nasal congestion. See also CATARRH, COMMON COLD, HAYFEVER, and INFLUENZA.

Treatment Catmint, Elderflower, Eyebright

> **Catmint** Painful congestion accompanied by thick catarrhal mucus.
>
> **Elderflower** Nasal inflammation and catarrh, the discharge occasionally linked with sneezing.
>
> **Eyebright** Watery, profuse catarrh with irritation, sneezing and often runny eyes.

Skin Problems

Mild problems of the skin often indicate excess toxic matter or general debility and respond to gently cleansing remedies – see also ACNE, BOILS. More complex conditions such as eczema or psoriasis may also be improved in this way, but really need qualified herbal treatment and advice.

Treatment Burdock, Chickweed, Nettle, Red Clover

> **Burdock** For inflamed skin conditions, especially when accompanied by pus-filled spots.
>
> **Chickweed** Use externally for soothing itchy, inflamed skin disorders.

Nettle Skin problems aggravated by tension and build up of toxins in the tissues.

Red Clover Also a tissue cleanser, improving quality of blood supply to the skin. Mild enough for use with children, in reduced dosages, and may be used externally to relieve excess inflammation.

Sore Throat

Inflammation of all or part of the throat with irritation ranging from mild tickling sensation to hoarseness, and often a difficulty in swallowing. See also LARYNGITIS and TONSILLITIS

Treatment Agrimony, Marshmallow, Sage, Thyme

Agrimony, Sage, Thyme These medicines have astringent properties, toning up the mucous membranes and are valuable as gargles, especially in tincture form. Also in this context, Tincture of Myrrh is strongly astringent. All used as mouthwashes or gargles.

Marshmallow Demulcent, soothing to the irritated membranes. May be used internally together with one of the above medicines to complement any gargle treatment.

Sprains   See FIRST AID SECTION

Sunburn   See FIRST AID SECTION

Thrush

An infection by the fungus Candida albicans; most common in the vagina or mouth. Becoming increasingly found in the bowel and throughout the whole system, largely due to disturbances in gut flora from many sources, such as antibiotics. Such widespread infection needs expert treatment as it often is a sign of lowered vitality and can herald serious illness.

Treatment Echinacea, Garlic, Marigold

> **Echinacea** Local use, especially of the diluted tincture, can be very helpful in combatting oral or vaginal thrush. Internally improves resistance to infections by stimulating immune system.
>
> **Garlic** Quite a powerful fungicidal remedy; improving the healthy bacteria population in the gut.
>
> **Marigold** Again, the diluted tincture may be used as a mouthwash or douche for local treatment.

Tonsillitis

Inflammation and infection of the tonsils, most often seen in children. There is pain and soreness on swallowing, which can be quite acute and may lead to an abscess or quinsy.

Treatment Agrimony, Echinacea, Garlic, Marshmallow, Sage

> **Agrimony, Sage** Use primarily as a gargle to tone the swollen, inflamed tonsils.
>
> **Echinacea, Garlic** Help build resistance to recurrent bouts of tonsillitis; for someone 'always picking up infections'. In such cases continue treatment for some weeks after an attack has passed.
>
> **Marshmallow** Soothing, internally and as a gargle, when there is pain on swallowing anything, even saliva.

Travel Sickness

Nausea or even vomiting caused by motion, such as on a boat or in a car. Helped by fresh air and by not looking down, for example reading whilst travelling.

Treatment Chamomile, Ginger, Peppermint

> These medicines can help to allay the discomfort and feelings of nausea. A useful method for ginger is to chew small pieces of the fresh root before and during travel.

Urinary Infections

Infection and inflammation of the lining of urinary tract, most commonly in the bladder – see CYSTITIS. Symptoms include a frequent urge to pass urine, and pain on doing so. The higher in the tract, the more likely is pain in the kidney area, possibly with fever and little urine. Kidney infections REQUIRE MEDICAL TREATMENT. Initial help for cystitis etc can be gained by increasing fluid intake.

Treatment Buchu, Chamomile, Marshmallow

> **Buchu** Take during mild infections and for a few weeks afterwards to heal damaged membranes.
>
> **Chamomile** For little flow of urine, with inflamed membranes. A hot infusion will be particularly relaxing.
>
> **Marshmallow** Eases pain and inflammation; useful to combine with more specifically anti-infective remedies such as **Buchu**.

Varicose Veins

Swollen veins in the legs, aggravated by long periods of standing. Combining rest with appropriate exercises to tone up the muscles and ease the congestion in the veins is helpful, but qualified treatment is likely to be necessary.

Treatment Lime Blossom, Marigold

> **Limeblossom** Helpful in toning the tissues of the blood vessels walls.
>
> **Marigold** External use as lotion or ointment to locally astringe the muscles and swollen veins.

Vomiting

May be due to a number of causes, mostly obvious and short-lived such as stomach infections, travel sickness, acute nervousness etc but could indicate more serious disorders. If prolonged or in doubt as to cause, Get Medical Aid.

Treatment **Balm, Chamomile, Peppermint**

> **Balm, Chamomile, Peppermint** These remedies can help to relax stomach muscles and relieve pressure to vomit. Also effective is Black Horehound (Ballota nigra).

Whooping Cough

Respiratory infection, most common in children, giving rise to a spasmodic cough with thick, sticky mucus and difficulty in breathing. Often, the effort to draw in air produces a 'Whooping' sound. In young children, this disease is potentially dangerous and **Qualified help should be sought**. Initial treatment can help to relax the tight airways and ease the cough.

Treatment **Chamomile, Horehound, Lavender, Thyme**

> **Chamomile** Eases distress and sleeplessness and lessens the nausea which may accompany bouts of coughing.
>
> **Horehound** For convulsive cough with the typical sticky mucus.
>
> **Lavender** Relaxing expectorant, removing mucus and calming generally.
>
> **Thyme** For harsh, unproductive cough with sore throat.

Wind See FLATULENCE

Herbal First Aid

Remember – if there is no improvement in the condition after a short period, seek qualified treatment or call a doctor for advice.

Bites and Stings

In all cases of bites and stings involving the mouth or throat, especially with any difficulty in breathing, get medical aid immediately.

Bee Stings
Remove the sting with tweezers. Cool the area with ice or cold compress.

Wasp Stings
Clean the area with lemon juice or vinegar, and cool as above.

Bites or Scratches
Clean the area thoroughly with water or surgical spirit.

Treatment Chamomile, Lavender, Red Clover

>Apply a cold dressing to the area, saturated with a solution of **Chamomile** infusion, or essential oil of **Lavender** to the area.

>Where there is itching and inflammation, a cool compress from **Red Clover** infusion may be applied. If itching persists, use Chickweed Ointment.

Bruises

Treatment Comfrey, Lavender, Witch Hazel

>**Comfrey** Where there is swelling, apply cold compress saturated in infusion of **Comfrey**. Later, or for minor bruises, apply Comfrey Ointment.
>
>**Lavender** Apply cold compress with essential oil of **Lavender** at rate of 5 drops to 1 tablespoon of cold water.
>
>**Witch Hazel** For swelling, with unbroken skin, use cold compress of distilled **Witch Hazel** at rate of 1 tablespoon to 1 pint of cold water.

Burns

Cool the area with cold running water for at least two minutes. For severe burns **refer immediately for medical aid**.

Treatment Lavender, Tea Tree

>After cooling the area, as above, apply 2–3 drops of essential oil of **Lavender** or of **Tea Tree**, to prevent blistering.

Cuts, Grazes etc

First of all clean the area gently but thoroughly to remove any dirt or grit. If the wound is severe enough to require dressing, just cover with a dry dressing and get medical aid.

Treatment Comfrey, Marigold, Witch Hazel, Yarrow

>**Comfrey** Use the ointment on minor cuts, scratches, grazes, and if necessary cover to keep clean.
>
>**Marigold** An alternative ointment to **Comfrey**, especially where there is inflammation and redness around the area.
>
>**Witch Hazel** Either wash with **Witch Hazel** or use it diluted, as for bruises, on a dressing to astringe cuts and minor wounds.
>
>**Yarrow** Use as compress or saturate a dressing to promote clotting and healing of cuts.

Fainting

Can be due to emotional shock, pain or hot, stuffy atmosphere. Ensure fresh air, loosen any tight clothing, place in comfortable position – lying down if possible. Use essential oil of **Lavender** held in front of face as smelling salts.

Nosebleed

Hold the soft part of the nose between finger and thumb, pinching firmly to stop the bleeding. Lean the head forward and continue to hold the nose for a few minutes. If available, use a cold compress of **Yarrow** to assist stopping the blood flow, placing small pad over bridge of the nose whilst pinching.

Scalds   See BURNS

Seasickness, Travel Sickness

See under MORNING SICKNESS and NAUSEA – SYMPTOM SECTION

Sprains and Strains

A **SPRAIN** is an injury affecting a joint, with torn ligaments and often much swelling eg ankle sprain.

A **STRAIN** is a muscular injury, primarily due to excessive exercise or incorrect use; there may be inflammation or just tenderness and stiffness.

Treatment Comfrey, Lavender, Rosemary

> **Comfrey** Use an infusion as a cold compress initially for sprains, to reduce the swelling. Then gently apply Comfrey Ointment to help speed healing. The ointment can also be rubbed into muscles strained through over-exercise.
>
> **Lavender** Use the essential oil as a cold compress for sprains, diluted at the rate of 5 drops to a tablespoon of cold water.

Rosemary Use the essential oil, preferably combined with essential oil of **Lavender**, to gently massage into aching muscles. It must be diluted, at the rate of 3 drops Rosemary oil plus 5 drops Lavender oil to 20ml (approx 1 tablespoon) of a vegetable oil such as Sweet Almond.

Stings   See BITES AND STINGS

Sunburn

Avoid any further exposure to the sun. Smaller areas in particular can be treated as for BURNS. If sunburn is mild but widespread, a cooling, moisturising cream can be helpful, especially if containing essential oils of Chamomile, Lavender or Tea Tree.

Wounds   See CUTS, GRAZES ETC

Herbal Medicines

This section gives more information on each herbal remedy and its applications to various ailments. Use in conjunction with the Symptoms Guide to find out the range of treatments available for your ailment. You do not have to experience *all* the symptoms listed under a medicine.

Of particular importance are dosage amounts; DO NOT EXCEED MAXIMUM DOSAGE LEVELS. See the section How to Select and Use **Herbal Medicines** for the method of taking the chosen remedy.

Agrimony (Agrimonia eupatoria)

This has an astringent effect on the digestive tract and is very useful for minor stomach irritations. Suitable for children's upsets or mild diarrhoea. It is a gentle bitter; improving liver function and toning the whole digestive system. The astringency of Agrimony makes it valuable for helping inflamed tissues, eg sore throats, to heal.

Ailments/ Symptoms	Cystitis
	Diarrhoea
	Dyspepsia
	Laryngitis
	Sore Throat
	Tonsillitis
Dosage	**0.5–2 grams three times a day**

Balm (Melissa officinalis)

Also called **Lemon Balm**, this is an excellent gentle relaxant and anti-spasmodic, relieving excessive tension and having an anti-depressant action. It should be thought of in stress-related problems, particularly for nervous indigestion, or during convalescence. A tea from the fresh leaves in particular is pleasant and refreshing.

Ailments/ Symptoms
Anxiety
Convalescence
Dyspepsia, especially with nervousness
Flatulence
Insomnia
Period problems

Dosage 1–3 grams three times a day

Buchu (Barosma betulina)

One of the best remedies for recurrent urinary infections such as cystitis. It is both a urinary antiseptic and diuretic, helping to remove irritating toxins which cause painful urination. It also has a soothing and healing effect on the inflamed surfaces and should be continued for a while after acute symptoms have gone.

Ailments/ Symptoms
Cystitis
Urinary infections

Dosage 0.5–2 grams three times a day

Burdock (Arctium lappa)

A cleansing alterative which helps the removal of potentially damaging waste matter through its diuretic and mildly laxative actions. For problems with accumulation of such matter eg chronic septic conditions, it is useful as a general cleanser. The root is quite powerful and dosage should start low and be gradually increased.

Ailments/ Symptoms
Acne
Boils
Skin problems, with inflammation

Dosage 0.5–2 grams three times a day

Catmint (Nepeta cataria)

Its sweat-inducing properties make this a highly useful medicine for colds and 'flu with feverishness, as it helps balance the circulation and also relieves nasal congestion. As a relaxant, **Catmint** is also valuable for indigestion and colicky pains.

Ailments/ Catarrh and nasal congestion
Symptoms Common Cold
Colic
Diarrhoea
Dyspepsia
Fever
Flatulence
Influenza
Sinusitis

Dosage **1–3 grams three times a day**

Cayenne (Capsicum minimum)

The strongest stimulant to the circulation and therefore of great value for conditions of cold, such as poor circulation in the hands or feet and even chilblains, or the early, shivering stages of a chill or cold. **Cayenne** also stimulates digestive secretions and can help weak digestion with flatulence; but AVOID where excess acid is produced in the stomach giving heartburn.

Ailments/ Chilblains
Symptoms Colic
Common Cold
Dyspepsia from debility and poor digestion
Flatulence
Influenza when feeling chilled and shivery
Poor circulation

Dosage **0.05–0.1 grams three times a day**

Chamomile (Chamomilla recutita)

The favourite remedy for home use for a variety of digestive upsets. It is an anti-spasmodic and carminative, relieving colicky pains and flatulence. As a gentle bitter it improves liver function and stimulates the digestion. Chamomile is anti-inflammatory with many uses, internally and externally. The relaxant effect also has wide application, helping problems like insomnia from worry or over-excitement and also period pains with muscle cramps. See children's section as well.

Ailments/ Symptoms	Biliousness
	Catarrh, particularly useful as a steam inhalation
	Colic
	Conjunctivitis
	Cystitis, easing inflammation and as a diuretic
	Diarrhoea
	Dyspepsia, perhaps use as an initial medicine for most digestive upsets
	Flatulence
	Hayfever, externally to ease the inflamed/irritated eyes
	Headaches, notably from indigestion and/or worry
	Insomnia
	Morning sickness
	Nausea
	Period problems
	Sciatica, to relieve muscle spasms and inflammation
	Travel sickness
	Urinary infections
	Whooping cough, helps calm spasmodic coughing and vomiting
Dosage	**0.5–3 grams three times a day**

Chickweed (Stellaria media)

This is a most soothing remedy for inflamed surfaces, used primarily EXTERNALLY for skin problems with irritation and itching, as an ointment or as a poultice.

Ailments/ Symptoms	Acne
	Boils
	Skin problems, including Dermatitis or Eczema where there is a lot of itching
Dosage	**Use either a commercial ointment or fresh plants to make a poultice**

Coltsfoot (Tussilago farfara)

A very effective expectorant, especially helpful in loosening a harsh, spasmodic cough and soothing the inflamed, irritated airways. Will also help to relax a nervous cough. Externally, a poultice can be very soothing for inflamed eruptions such as boils or carbuncles.

Ailments/ Boils, as an external remedy
Symptoms Bronchitis, particularly with dry, spasmodic cough
Cough

Dosage **0.5–1 gram (flower preparations)**
1–2 grams (leaf preparations)
Three times a day

Comfrey (Symphytum officinale)

Probably the best healing agent as a local application for cuts, grazes, wounds, even ulcers. The ointment is likely to be the major external treatment for domestic use. *There have been doubts (unsubstantiated) raised over the safety of Comfrey in long term high dosage* internally, but short-term use offers relatively safe, effective treatment for soothing inflamed mucus membranes, for example in bronchitis or gastric upsets. External use is completely safe.

Ailments/ Bronchitis
Symptoms Bruises
Cuts, grazes etc
Dyspepsia, especially with mild diarrhoea
Haemorrhoids, external application
Sprains

Dosage **0.5–2 grams three times a day**

Dandelion (Taraxacum officinale)

Almost two medicines derived from one plant; the leaf is a strong diuretic, with a naturally high potassium content which replaces that lost in the extra urine passed; the root is more active as a gentle laxative and liver tonic. This latter effect gives **Dandelion** a wide medicinal application since the liver is often placed under considerable stress through lifestyle, dietary and environmental imbalances.

Ailments/ Acne
Symptoms Biliousness
Boils
Constipation
Cystitis
Dyspepsia, with sluggish digestion
Rheumatism

Dosage 1–4 grams (leaf preparations)
1–3 grams (root preparations)
Three times a day

Echinacea (Echinacea angustifolia)

Very effective in increasing the ability of the immune system to fight infections, it is a stimulating alterative for use in helping cleanse the body in septic conditions or where resistance to infections is lowered. For people who feel sluggish, cold and lacking in vitality.

Ailments/ Symptoms Abscess
Acne
Boils
Cystitis
Influenza
Laryngitis, also as a gargle
Thrush
Tonsillitis

Dosage 0.5–1 gram three times a day

Elderflower (Sambucus nigra)

This has a stong diaphoretic effect, regulating the body temperature in feverish conditions (especially when used as hot infusion) and cleansing the system by increased sweating. As a diuretic, increasing urination which also helps detoxify the body. Especially for colds etc with nasal congestion and catarrh; improves the circulation and relieves sinus pressure.

Ailments/ Symptoms Catarrh
Common Cold
Fever
Influenza
Poor circulation
Sinusitis

Dosage 1–3 grams three times a day

Eyebright (Euphrasia officinalis)

The astringent and anti-inflammatory properties of **Eyebright** make it a valuable medicine to improve inflamed sinuses and also as an external aid for mild conjunctivitis or eyelid inflammation. It can give considerable relief to hay fever sufferers who have itchy, sore eyes and watery nasal catarrah or sneezing. For external use, make an infusion and when cooled apply on cotten wool pads as a compress (or use a cooled, strained decoction as an eyebath).

Ailments/ Catarrh, particularly with runny, watery mucus and nasal congestion
Symptoms Conjunctivitis, externally but seek medical advice if it continues
Eye problems, with inflammation or soreness, used externally
Hay fever
Sinusitis

Dosage **1–3 grams three times a day.**

Feverfew
(Chrysanthemum parthenium; also known as Tanacetum parthenium)

Has experienced great popularity recenty for use by migraine sufferers. Where the blood vessels have become severely restricted it acts to relax them and ease the accompanying pain and inflammation. Most migraines fit this pattern and are usually relieved by applying local warmth to the head. As a bitter, **Feverfew** stimulates sluggish digestion, itself often a cause of headaches. The anti-inflammatory effect may be useful in an acute flare-up of arthritis. DO NOT USE IN PREGNANCY. Occasionally **Feverfew** produces mouth ulcers, if so avoid contact of the herb with the lining of the mouth.

Ailments/ Biliousness and poor digestion
Symptoms Headaches
Migraine

Dosage **1 leaf or powdered equivalent. Best taken fresh three times a day**

Garlic (Allium sativum)

A powerfully cleansing remedy, particularly effective in preventing or treating digestive and respiratory infections. Taken over a period, it helps to lower blood cholesterol levels and blood pressure (but seek qualified treatment). To improve resistance to recurrent colds, catarrh or bronchial infections take daily throughout the winter months. The maximum effect is gained by eating raw garlic but the perles/tablets are less anti-social!

Ailments/   Bronchitis and bronchial infections
Symptoms   Catarrh
Common Cold
Cystitis
Dyspepsia from digestive infections
– garlic can repeat badly on some people
Fever
Influenza
Poor circulation
Thrush, including fungal infections in the gut
Tonsillitis

Dosage   **1–2 cloves of raw garlic, or 1 perle three times a day**

Ginger (Zingiber officinale)

Warming for the whole system, improves the circulation to the extremities. Relieves spasm in the digestive tract, very effective for colic and flatulent indigestion. Excellent in the cold, shivery stages of colds or influenza, especially taken as a hot infusion.

Ailments/   Bronchitis, particulary during cold, damp weather
Symptoms   Colic and cramping pains
Dyspepsia with wind and painful bloating of abdomen
Flatulence
Influenza
Morning sickness
Poor circulation
Rheumatism, improves circulation through the affected areas
Travel sickness

Dosage   **0.25–0.5 gram three times a day**

Horehound (Marrubium vulgare)

A traditional cough medicine, relaxing to the bronchial muscles and acting as an expectorant to loosen thick sticky mucus. It is particularly of use in relieving a spasmodic cough with congestion but little shifting of phlegm – valuable for example in whooping cough (but seek qualified advice and treatment). As a bitter it stimulates digestion and improves liver function.

Ailments/   Biliousness
Symptoms   Bronchitis
               Cough
               Dyspepsia with sluggish digestion
               Whooping cough

Dosage   0.5–1 gram three times a day

Hyssop (Hyssopus officinalis)

A relaxing expectorant medicine, valuable to give relief from colds, coughs and chestiness associated with tension and nervousness or agitation. Its gentle calming and anti-spasmodic effects help problems of anxiousness generally.

Ailments/   Anxiety
Symptoms   Bronchitis
               Catarrh
               Common cold
               Cough
               Fever
               Influenza
               Insomnia
               Poor circulation

Dosage   1–2 grams three times a day

Lavender (Lavandula officinalis)

A warming relaxant medicine which relieves muscle spasms whilst also having a marked anti-depressant action. The aromatic essential oil is an excellent local tissue-healer and antiseptic. Internally, **Lavender** is particularly suited to conditions associated with tension and/or depression.

Ailments/ Symptoms	Anxiety
	Bronchitis with tightness in the chest and tension
	Burns
	Colic
	Depression
	Dyspepsia
	Dyspepsia with gas and bloating, especially from nervousness
	Headaches
	Insomnia
	Nervous problems, including irritability and exhaustion
	Muscular aches and pains, muscle cramps
	Rheumatism
	Sciatica
	Shingles
	Whooping cough
Dosage	0.5–1 gram three times a day. For muscular or rheumatic aches etc, use the essential oil externally, diluted at 1–3% in a vegetable oil (i.e. 1–3 drops per 5ml teaspoon of vegetable oil) and gently massage in

Lime Blossom (Tilia europaea)

A soothing relaxant, ideal for problems associated with nervous tension as it calms without sedating. Also improves circulation to the extremities and is a mild diaphoretic, being valuable in feverish conditions such as influenza, with restlessness or insominia. Used by qualified herbal practitioners for cardiovascular problems associated with anxiety or stress.

Ailments/ Symptoms	Anxiety
	Colds
	Dyspepsia with nervousness lending to slight looseness of bowels
	Fever
	Headaches, especially from tension
	Influenza, good for children who cannot settle down to sleep due to 'flu
	Insomnia
	Nervous problems stemming from raised tension levels
	Poor circulation
	Varicose veins
Dosage	1–3 grams three times a day

Marigold (Calendula officinalis)

As an external remedy **Calendula** has a good reputation and many domestic uses, particularly for skin conditions where there is inflammation, whether from wounds, grazes or minor burns (see FIRST AID SECTION) or even dermatitis, eczema and the like (but seek qualified herbal treatment). Internally, **Calendula** is an astringent, anti-inflammatory medicine, healing damaged mucous membranes in the stomach, or digestive inflammation.

Ailments/ Symptoms
- Burns
- Conjunctivitis, as an eyepad
- Cuts, grazes etc
- Dyspepsia, stomach pains affected by intake of food or drink
- Haemorrhoids, local application
- Mouth ulcers, use tincture as a gargle
- Thrush
- Varicose veins, local application

Dosage 0.5–2 grams three times a day

Marshmallow (Althaea officinalis)

One of the best medicines for calming painful, irritated or inflamed surfaces, both externally and internally. Its high mucilage content is very soothing and, whilst not directly healing, this helps the body's defences to get to work on repairing damaged tissue. A safe remedy for children and infants, easing bronchial or gastric inflammation.

Ailments/ Symptoms
- Acne, local application (poultice or compress)
- Boils, as above
- Bronchitis, with thick catarrh and irritating cough
- Cough
- Cystitis, burning sensation and irritability
- Dyspepsia
- Laryngitis
- Sore throat
- Urinary infections

Dosage 2–4 grams three times a day

Meadowsweet (Filipendula ulmaria)

Analgesic and anti-inflammatory medicine, partly due to its salicylate content – unlike synthetic sources such as aspirin this is balanced in **Meadowsweet** by other healing plant constituents so as to be soothing to the stomach wall and other surfaces. Its astringency makes it valuable in relieving mild diarrhoea, including children's looseness. The anti-inflammatory effect helps in a variety of conditions.

Ailments/ Symptoms
- Cystitis
- Diarrhoea, associated with mild gastric upsets
- Dyspepsia, including overproduction of acid and heartburn
- Morning sickness
- Rheumatism

Nettle (Urtica dioica)

A gentle but effective alterative, cleansing the tissue of waste products. A dietary and circulatory stimulant. All these properties gave **Nettle** a traditional reputation as a spring tonic and cleanser, with its high mineral content, including iron. Useful for many problems, from skin infections and imbalance to rheumatic disorders.

Ailments/ Symptoms
- Acne
- Boils
- Eczema, but seek qualified herbal treatment
- Poor circulation
- Rheumatism
- Skin problems, associated with high levels of toxic waste products and/or chronic stress

Dosage **1–3 grams three times a day**

Oats (Avena Sativa)

Medicinally, the wild oat is used; it is the finest remedy for nervous exhaustion, debility, depression or convalescence, acting slowly but steadily to restore normal nervous functioning, without any overstimulation. Since excessive, prolonged or inappropriate stress is a part of many people's lives, this medicine has wide-spread applications.

Ailments/ Anxiety, especially chronic states of tension
Symptoms Nervous problems in general
Shingles

Dosage 1–3 grams three times a day

Peppermint (Mentha piperita)

Long-standing reputation as a medicine to relieve digestive spasms and calm the stomach. This anti-spasmodic action is combined with a cooling effect and increased sweating which makes **Peppermint** very helpful in relieving and improving feverish colds, 'flu etc

Ailments/ Colic
Symptoms Common Cold
Dyspepsia with spasmodic pains
Fever
Flatulence
Headaches due to tension and/or digestive upset
Influenza
Morning sickness
Nausea
Period problems
Travel sickness

Dosage **0.5–2 grams three times a day**

Raspberry Leaf (Rubus idaeus)

Acting as a gentle tonic to the uterus, the prime use of this medicine is to promote an easier, more efficient labour. As an astringent, **Raspberry Leaf** is also of value in conditions such as laryngitis or tonsillitis, or digestive upsets with diarrhoea. For use in pregnancy to improve labour, take in gradually increasing doses during the last two months of the pregnancy.

Ailments/ Laryngitis
Symptoms Pregnancy – not an ailment!, take as described above
Tonsillitis, especially as a gargle

Dosage **1–4 grams three times a day**

Red Clover (Trifolium pratense)

An alterative remedy, cleansing the system yet mild enough for many children's skin problems, even eczema – but individual treatment is essential in complex conditions. A lotion of **Red Clover** used externally can give relief from itching in skin disorders.

Ailments/ Acne
Symptoms Boils and similar eruptions
Cough, helps to loosen a dry, spasmodic cough
Eczema, but see note above
Skin problems especially with irritation

Dosage 1–3 grams three times a day

Rosemary (Rosemarinus officinalis)

Improves nervous function, stimulates the circulation and is a gentle liver tonic. **Rosemary** is an excellent medicine for use in situations where there is exhaustion or debility, even depression following a period of stress. It is also a local circulatory stimulant and can be used on flakey scalps – either by infusion or a few drops of essential oil massaged in well before rinsing.

Ailments/ Anxiety, leading to fatigue
Symptoms Biliousness
Convalescence
Dyspepsia, with sluggish digestion
Flatulence
Hair problems, including flaking and dandruff – see above
Headache
Migraine
Muscular aches and pains – see under
Lavender for dilution rates for external use
Nervous problems, including depression and exhaustion
Poor circulation
Shingles

Dosage 0.5–2 grams three times a day

Sage (Salvia officinalis)

An astringent and antiseptic medicine, highly recommended for treating soreness and inflammation in the throat or mouth, both as a gargle and for internal use; but AVOID INTERNALLY IN PREGNANCY. **Sage** also has some value in relieving indigestion with gas or spasmodic pains.

Ailments/ Laryngitis
Symptoms Mouth ulcers, infections generally in the mouth
Sore throat
Tonsillitis

Dosage **0.5–1.5 grams, Sage** is especially helpful as a gargle – the tincture is best. If not, an infusion will help
Three times a day

Slippery Elm (Ulmus fulva)

Very soothing, suitable for all digestive inflammation and discomfort. Being easily absorbed it is ideal for use during convalescence, when the appetite is poor and digestion inadequate. Externally, a poultice can be applied to skin eruptions with inflammation; **Slippery Elm** is widely available in powder form which is ideal for this.

Ailments/ Acne Use a poultice.
Symptoms Boils mix powdered **Slippery elm** with hot water
Convalescence, as a dietary aid
Diarrhoea, soothing and mildly astringent
Dyspepsia with inflammation and soreness

Dosage **2–5 grams Three times a day**

Thyme (Thymus vulgaris)

The antiseptic action of **Thyme**, concentrated in its aromatic essential oil, combined with spasm-relieving and expectorant properties, make it powerfully effective in combatting respiratory infections. It is of particular benefit where there is a harsh, tense, dry cough. For sore throats etc, a gargle is very helpful. Finally, mild gastric infections with accompanying diarrhoea will respond well to **Thyme**.

Ailments/ Symptoms	Bronchitis, with harsh coughing
	Cough
	Diarrhoea and stomach upsets
	Dyspepsia
	Flatulence
	Laryngitis
	Mouth ulcers
	Sore throats and infections, especially as a gargle
	Whooping cough
Dosage	0.5–3 grams three times a day

Valerian (Valeriana officinalis)

A strong relaxant and anti-spasmodic, with only mild sedative effects. The relaxation is also helpful in improving warmth and circulation where tension produces feelings of cold. Do not use for indefinitely, if problems are persisting, see a qualified practitioner.

Ailments/ Symptoms	Anxiety
	Colic
	Constipation due to tension and a 'spastic colon'
	Cramps
	Headaches from tension
	Insomnia for same reason
	Migraines
	Nervous problems, where anxiety is the most important factor
	Period problems with cramping pains
	Sciatica
Dosage	Dosage 1–3 grams three times a day

Witch Hazel (Hamamelis virginiana)

Strongly astringent (less so in the commonly found distilled form), it is a traditional external remedy for cuts (see FIRST AID SECTION) Also highly valuable applied locally to haemorrhoids, swellings and bruises. Internally it can give relief in diarrhoea and digestive inflammation.

Ailments/ Bruises (see FIRST AID Cut, wounds SECTION)
Symptoms Diarrhoea
Haemorrhoids, locally as a cream or lotion
Varicose veins, locally as above

Dosage **0.5–2 grams three times a day**

Yarrow (Achillea millefolium)

Another traditional healing agent for wounds. Internally, it helps improve circulation to the extremities, stimulates digestion and induces sweating – very useful in treating feverish colds or 'flu. The effect on the circulation can act to lower blood pressure, not an area for self-treatment but an effect to be aware of if taken for some time.

Ailments/ Chilblains
Symptoms Cuts, wounds etc (see FIRST AID SECTION)
Colds
Cystitis, increases flow of urine and reduces inflammation
Dyspepsia with poor digestion, often as part of a reaction to an infection
Fever
Influenza, especially where feverish
Poor circulation

Dosage **1–3 grams three times a day**

Herbal Medicines Particularly Appropriate for Children's Ailments

Generally speaking, children's and adult's symptoms should be considered in the same way, and the medical herbalist will of course treat children individually in any case. Some herbal remedies are particularly suited for children and their reactions to illness, and they are indicated, with suggested uses, in this section.

Balm
A gently relaxing remedy suitable for a wide variety of children's problems. Especially nervous indigestion and during the convalescent stage of illnesses. A tea from the fresh leaves is particularly pleasant to take and may be used cold in the summer.

Catmint
For the child who suffers from frequent colds, blocked ears and sinus congestion, especially if there is some feverishness and perhaps a lack of appetite.

Chamomile
Probably the first herb to think of for most digestive upsets, ranging from nausea through stomach pains and flatulence to mild diarrhoea. It is particularly valuable for children who get upset when they are ill or react peevishly and crossly.

Elderflower
Childhood catarrh and sinusitis can often be relieved by **Elderflower** especially if feverish but not sweating very well, also if feeling quite cold, as it is a good temperature regulator.

Garlic

Only for those (probably older) children who can tolerate it! If the child suffers from frequent respiratory, or perhaps digestive, infections then the regular use of garlic can be very helpful in building resistance and easing nasal congestion or catarrh. Probably the perles, at a low dose, will be the easiest method.

Hyssop

For coughs, colds or influenza, especially if the child is unable to sleep or gets agitated by the symptoms. Relaxes the airways and helps removal of sticky phlegm whilst gently calming overall.

Lime Blossom

Another mild relaxant, easing pain and discomfort and applicable for many childhood diseases, from headaches to colds/flu to stomach upsets. Will help to induce a restful sleep, aiding recovery from illness.

Peppermint

A valuable antispasmodic for colicky pains, flatulence and other symptoms of digestive disorder. Good for children who have over-eaten. Also helpful in chills or influenza when shivering is followed by hot, restless feelings.

Other herbal medicines discussed in this book can also be of considerable value in particular ailments – see both Herbal Medicines and Symptoms sections. In all situations when treating children REMEMBER to adjust the dosage (See How to Select and Use Herbal Medicines) and IF SYMPTOMS PERSIST OR GET WORSE CONSULT A QUALIFIED PRACTITIONER OR YOUR DOCTOR.

Veterinary Herbal Medicine

Generally, animals respond extremely well to herbal medicine. This is scarcely surprising, since herbal treatment has worked for people and animals over many centuries, and many wild animals will instinctively seek out plants necessary for their healing properties. A vestige of this behaviour can be seen in domesticated cats or dogs eating grass to make themselves sick if they are unwell from some food.

Provided that an owner knows the animal well, and remembers to adjust dosage to the size of the animal, it is perfectly feasible for minor ailments to be treated effectively and safely at home using one of the veterinary herbal remedies available. External applications such as ointments/compresses can be used, as discussed in the First Aid section, with equally good results. Obviously, if in doubt consult a veterinary surgeon. For further information there are a few books available which deal with herbal medicine for animals – the best advice is to go to a good book shop and browse through the book to see if it deals with your type of animal.

Glossary of Terms in Common Use

Acute An illness which has a short duration but may well have quite severe symptoms during that time. A term usually used in contrast to the term chronic (see below).

Adaptogen Gradually becoming more used in connection with herbal medicine. This term was originally applied to those herbal remedies which helped our responses to stress situations, improving our ability to adapt and cope (for example Ginseng. Nowadays, the term is used to describe herbal remedies which help to restore balance to a system and can thus help in seemingly opposing conditions.

Alterative A difficult term to define; the modern equivalent of 'blood-cleanser' gives rather more clues to its meaning. Basically, herbal alteratives improve the supply of nutrients to and elimination of toxins from all the tissues in the body. Often they are of most value in long-term conditions with an excess of toxic wastes, such as rheumatic disorders or skin problems.

Astringent Term applied to herbal medicines which lessen the irritability of mucous membranes and reduce inflammation. This lessening of irritability can be valuable for example in treating diarrhoea. The effect is usually brought about by tannins in the medicine, chemicals which produce a temporary leathery coating to the surface of the digestive tract.

Bitters	Medicines with a definite bitter taste which reflexly act to stimulate digestive juices and bile flow, and improve the appetite. As such they were traditionally used as tonics and have widespread applications today.
Carminative	A term applied to remedies which ease flatulence and/or colicky symptoms due to excess gas.
Chronic	An illness which lasts for long periods of time, the symptoms may have been consistent or have recurred at intervals, with acute flare-ups.
Convalescence	A feature of illness considered more important by herbalists than is usually the case in orthodox medicine. The recovery stages require energy to be conserved and the whole system gently restored to normal functioning.
Demulcents	Medicines which have a soothing effect on the surfaces or membranes to which they are administered. Often the medicines contain a lot of mucilage which gives a slimy coating and eases inflammation.
Diaphoretics	Remedies that produce sweating, mostly noticeable if one is actually feverish.
Essential oils	The concentrated essences produced by methods such as steam distillation. These volatile oils often contain considerable therapeutic actions. Because of their intense concentration they should ONLY be used internally by a qualified medical herbalist. For external use these oils are usually diluted.
Infusion	A preparation made by steeping the herb in hot water. Having poured boiling water over the plant material, cover and leave for 5–10 minutes before straining. Can be kept in a fridge for 3–4 days only.
Nervines	More usually termed nervous restoratives, such remedies have a generally supportive, nourishing action on the nervous system. They have many uses, in conditions of fatigue or exhaustion especially.

Relaxant A term used to describe the action of many herbal medicines, and intended as a distinction from sedative or tranquillising drugs; relaxants are sometimes described as calming 'from the neck down', and are helpful wherever irritability or muscle spasm is involved.

Stimulant In herbal medicine, a term describing a remedy which increases the activity of a system but without building up energy reserves. This activity can be very positive in improving the body's attempts to restore health but for debilitated people the use of nervines as well, or instead, will be more helpful to prevent further exhaustion.

Tincture A preparation made by steeping the herb in an alcohol/water mixture, normally for up to two weeks. This method often extracts more constituents from the plant material than by infusion and produces a concentrated, long-lasting medicine.

ORGANISATIONS

In the UK

BRITISH HERBAL MEDICINE ASSOCIATION

An umbrella organisation for manufacturers and suppliers of herbal medicines, and practitioners. The BHMA seeks to maintain standards for the trade and represents their interests in discussions with the Department of Health. It also publishes the British Herbal Pharmacopoeia which is the standard reference for macroscopical/microscopial definitions of medicinal plants and their therapeutic indications.

British Herbal Medicine Association
PO Box 304
Bournemouth
Dorset BH7 6JZ
Tel: 0202 433691

GENERAL COUNCIL AND REGISTER OF CONSULTANT HERBALISTS

This Association keeps a register of its members who take a part-time correspondence course in herbal medicine. It also oversees their codes of ethics and practice as well as the training itself, through the Faculty of Herbal Medicine.

General Council and Register of Consultant Herbalists
Marlborough House
Swanpool
Falmouth
Cornwall TR11 4HW
Tel: 0326 317321

THE HERB SOCIETY

Originally founded in 1927 as a society for practitioners/suppliers; the Herb Society was registered as an educational charity in 1976. A lay organisation open to anyone interested in the uses or growing of herbs, the Society has a library of books on herbs and publishes a quarterly journal, The Herbal Review, free to subscribing members.

The Herb Society
77 Great Peter Street
London SW1P 2EI
Tel: 01 222 3634

NATIONAL INSTITUTE OF MEDICAL HERBALISTS

Established in 1864, the NIMH is the oldest professional body of herbal practitioners in the world. It publishes a Register of Members, who must be graduates from the School of Herbal Medicine, and who adhere to strict codes of ethics and practice. The NIMH provides the therapeutic information for the British Herbal Pharmacopoeia and conducts research on behalf of its members. It produces an information leaflet for the public and publishes an in-house journal, the New Herbal Practitioner.

National Institute of Medical Herbalists
41 Hatherley Road
Winchester
Hampshire SO22 6RR
Tel: 0962 68776

SCHOOL OF HERBAL MEDICINE

Linked to the National Institute of Medical Herbalists to which its graduates may apply for Membership, the School runs a 4 year full-time course and a 4 year part-time tutorial course. Allied to the School is the College of Phytotherapy which is an information and research centre.

School of Herbal Medicine
Bucksteep Manor
Bodle Street Green
Hailsham
E. Sussex BN27 4RJ
Tel: 0323 833812

In the U.S.A.

THE AMERICAN HERB ASSOCIATION
P.O Box 353,
Rescue, CA 95672

THE SCHOOL OF HERBAL MEDICINE

Offers correspondence course. For information send S.A.S.E. to:

P.O. Box 168–G
Suquamish,
WA 98392

THE HERB RESEARCH FOUNDATION

A non-profit research and educational organization dedicated to raising funds, and providing reliable research data to members, the public and the press.

P.O. Box 2602
Longmont, CO 80501
Tel: 303/449–2265

In Australia

NATIONAL HERBALISTS ASSOCIATION OF AUSTRALIA
P.O. Box,
Kingsgrove,
NSW 2208

Suppliers

There is an increasing number of companies manufacturing or supplying herbal medicines, or the plant material itself for medicinal use. The following are a selection of the most widely available, reputable sources.

ARKOPHARMA (UK) LIMITED

Individual herb tablets, available in many outlets.

Exchange House
Hindhead Road, Hindhead
Surrey GU26 6AD
Tel: 042873 6442

CULPEPER

A number of shops across the country, also by mail order. Supplies dried herbs in small amounts and some tablets.

Hadstock Road
Linton, Cambridge CB1 6NJ
Tel: 0223 891196

DENES VETERINARY HERBAL PRODUCTS LTD

Major suppliers of veterinary herbal medications, available in many outlets.

14 Goldstone Street
Hove, East Sussex BN3 3RL
Tel: 0273 25364

GERARD HOUSE LTD

Supplier of individual and combination herb tablets, widely available.

3 Wickham Road
Bournemouth, Dorset BH7 6JX
Tel: 0202 434116

POTTER'S HERBAL SUPPLIES LTD

Long-standing major supplier of dried herbs, individual and combination herbal medicines widely available.

Leyland Mill Lane
Wigan, Lancashire WN1 2SB
Tel: 0942 34761

In the U.S.A.

POTTERS HERBAL SUPPLIES

The U.S. agent is;

Regent Bond Ltd
159 W. 53rd Street
Suite 35H,
New York,
N.Y. 10019

Suggestions for Further Reading

THE HOLISTIC HERBAL
David Hoffman

A comprehensive account of the approach to health of herbal medicine and the actions of herbs. Includes a traditional herbal outlining the description, indications and dosages of medicinal plants.

Findhorn Press

THE DICTIONARY OF MODERN HERBALISM
Simon Mills

An A–z of plants, illnesses and terms used in herbal practice, with definitions and cross-references. Of interest to lay-person and professional alike.

Thorsons

ALTERNATIVES IN HEALING
The Author and others; Consultant Editor, Simon Mills

An account of six major therapies, including orthodox medicine, with comparisons of their approach to particular health problems. Highlights the major role that herbal medicine has to offer in our choice of health care.

Macmillan

GREEN PHARMACY
Barbara Griggs

A fascinating look at the history of herbal medicine. Not a guide to medicinal actions but clearly showing some of the personalities and influences who have helped maintain and shape herbalism through the centuries.

Jill Norman and Hobhouse

POTTER'S NEW CYCLOPAEDIA OF BOTANICAL DRUGS AND PREPARATIONS
R.C. Wren and completely revised by
Elizabeth M. Williamson, BSc, PhD, MR PharmS, FLS and Fred J. Evans, DSc, B Pharm, PhD, MR PharmS, FLS, MNIMH (Hon)

A referenced cyclopaedia giving the uses, preparations, doses, synonyms and distinctive characters of all botanical drugs used in medicine.

The C.W. Daniel Company Ltd

INDEX

Abscess 23
Achillea millefolium see Yarrow
acidity, excess 11
acne 23
'active constituent' 11
Act of Parliament, 1968 Medicines 12–13, 15
acute 75
adaptogen 75
Agrimony (*Agrimonia eupatoria*) 53
    catarrh 26
    cystitis 30
    diarrhoea 31
    dyspepsia 32
    throat affection 38, 44, 45
Allergic Rhinitis 35
Allium sativum see Garlic
alterative 54, 58, 64
    definition 75
alternative treatment 11
Althaea officinalis see Marshmallow
analgesic 64
animal, treatment of 18, 73
anti-depressant 53–4, 61
anti-inflamatory 55, 59, 63, 64
anti-spasmodic 53, 55, 60, 61, 65, 67, 68
antibiotics 44
antiseptic 54, 61, 66, 67
anxiety 24
Arctium lappa 54
    constipation 29
    skin problem 25, 43
aspirin 11
asthma 35
astringent 53, 59, 63–6 *passim*, 68
    definition 75

athletes foot 24
Avena sativa see Oats

back pain 42
balance of compounds 11
Balbota nigra 47
Balm (Lemon Balm; *Melissa officinalis*) 53–4
    anxiety 24
    child ailment 71
    convalescence 29
    digestive disorder 32, 34
    insomnia 37
    period problems 41
    vomiting 47
bark (herb) preparation 22 (table)
Barosma betulina 54
    uses 31, 46
bite 49
bitter 59, 61
    definition 76
    gentle 53, 55
Black Horehound (*Balbota nigra*) 47
bladder inflamation 30
bleeding, stomach lining of 11
blood
    cholesterol level 59
    pressure 35, 59, 69
    sugar levels, low 39
boil 25
bronchitis 25–6
bruise 50
burn 50
Buchu (*Barosma betulina*) 54

uses 31, 46
Burdock (*Arctium lappa*) 54
   constipation 29
   skin problem 26, 43

Candida albicans (fungus) 44
Capsicum minimum see Cayenne
carbuncle (boil) 25
cardiovascular problem 62
carminative 55
   definition 76
carrier oil 52
'case' 10
catarrh 26–7
Catmint (*Nepeta cataria*) 54–5
   catarrh/sinusitis 26, 43
   child ailment 71
   colic 31
   fever 33
   indigestion 27, 34
   influenza 36
cause of ill-health 23
Cayenne (*Capsicum minimum*) 55
   bronchitis 25
   chilblains 27
   digestive disorder 34
   influenza 36
   poor circulation 41
Chamomile (*Chamomilla recutia*) 55–6
   anxiety 24
   bite/sting 49
   bowel disorder 29, 31
   child ailment 71
   conjunctivitis 28
   digestive disorder 27, 32, 34
   hayfever 35
   nausea/vomiting 39, 45, 47
   sciatica 42
   women, beneficial to 38–41 *passim*
   urinary infection 31, 46
   whooping cough 47
Chamomile, essential oil of 52
'change of life' 38
chickenpox virus 43
Chickweed (*Stellaria media*) 56
   uses 43; of ointment 49
chilblains 27
child, treatment of
   appropriate herbs 25, 53, 63, 66
   particularly 71–2
   dosage 16, 17, 22
Chrysanthemum parthenium 59
   migraine use 38
circulation (poor) 41
   indication of 27
   strongest stimulant 55
cleanser 54, 58, 59, 64, 66
cold, common 28
colic 27
Coltsfoot (*Tussilago farfora*) 56–7
   cough 25, 30
Comfrey (*Symphytum officinale*) 57
   cough 25, 30
   cut/graze 50
   haemorrhoids 35
   sprain/strain 51
Comfrey ointment 50
common cold 28
compress, cold 50, 51
conjunctivitis 28
constipation 28–9
   chronic 34
consultation 16
convalescence 29
cooling effect 65
cough 29–30
   dry, spasmodic 26
   painful 25, 26
   whooping 47
cramping pains, spasmodic *see also* period problems
Culpeper, Nicholas 9
cut 50
cystitis 30–1; see also urinary infection

Dandelion (*Taraxacum officinale*) 57–8
   uses 32, 42
debility 41
   indication of 39
demulcent 76

depression **41**
diaphoretic **33, 58, 62**
   definition **76**
diarrhoea **31–2**
diet improvement **34**
dietary
   fibre lack **28**
   intolerance **23**
digestive disorder **32, 34, 67**
   favourite remedy for **55**
diuretic **54, 57, 58**
dressing **49, 50**
drugs, herbal medication with **17**
dyspepsia **32**

earache **33**
Echinacea (*Echinacea augustifolia*) **58**
   boil **25**
   cystitis **31**
   influenza **36**
   laryngitis **38**
   thrush **45**
eczema **35, 43**
Egyptian **9**
Elderflower (*Sambucus niger*) **58**
   catarrh/sinusitis **26, 43**
   child ailment **71**
   cold/influenza **28, 36**
   fever **33**
   poor circulation **41**
elderly person, frail, treatment of
   bronchitis **25**
   dosage **22**
   influenza **36**
   poor circulation **41**
   shingles **43**
elimination **42**
essential oil **36, 39**
   definition **76**
   First Aid uses **49–52**
Euphrasia officinalis see Eyebright
expectorant **56, 60, 61, 67**
eye
   inflamation **28**
   pad/bath **33, 35**
   problems **33**
   puffiness under **26**
   smarting **35**
Eyebright (*Euphrasia officinalis*) **59**
   catarrh/sinusitis **26, 43**
   conjunctivitis **28**
   hayfever **35**

fainting **51**
feet, cold **41**
fever **33**
Feverfew (*Tanacetum parthenium* or
      Chrysanthemum parthenium) **59**
   migraine use **38**
Filipendula ulmaria see Meadowsweet
finger, swelling on **27**
First Aid, herbal **49–52**
flatulence **34**
flower (herb) preparation **22** (table)
foot, athletes **24**

gargle **39, 44, 67**
Garlic (*Allium sativum*) **59–60**
   bronchitis **26**
   child ailment **72**
   cystitis **31**
   fever **33**
   influenza **36**
   poor circulation **41**
   thrush **45**
gastric problem **11**
gastritis (dyspepsia) **32**
Ginger (*Zingiber officinale*) **60**
   bronchitis **25**
   chilblains **27**
   cold/influenza **28, 36**
   digestive disorder **27, 34**
   poor circulation **41**
   rheumatism **42**
   sickness **39, 45**
glandular fever **29**
grass eating **73**
graze **50**

Greek 9
groin irritation/itch 24

haemorrhoids 34–5
Hamamelis virginiana 68–9
  diarrhoea 32
  haemorrhoids 35
  cut/graze 50
hands, cold 41
hayfever (allergic rhinitis) 35
headache 35–6
  severe (migraine) 38–9
healing agent 57
heartburn (dyspepsia) 11, 32, 55
herb
  preparation, home 22 (table)
  tea 28, 54
herbal medicine
  definition 9
  development 9–10
  modern practice 11–13
  origins 9–10
  practitioners/organizations 15, 79–81
  principles 10–11
  questions/answers concerning 15–18
  suppliers 83–4
  terms, common use in 75–7
  veterinary 18, 73
herbal medicines (remedies) 53–71
  common use in 19–20
  dosage 21, 22; *see also* individual herbs
  drugs taken alongside 17
  effectiveness 15
  homoeopathy compared 18
  methods of taking 16–17, 21
  preparation, home 22 (table)
  reaction/result 17
  safety 15
  selection/use 21–2; *see also* individual herbs
  storage 16
    home preparations 22
  symptoms guide 23–52; *see also* individual herbs
  treatment of:
    animal 18, 73
    child *see* child, treatment of
    elderly person *see* elderly person, frail, treatment of
    self 21–2
herbal medicines, general remedy 18
'Herbalists Charter' 12
Hippocrates 9
home preparation 22 (table)
homoeopathy 18
Horehound (*Marrubium vaulgare*) 60–1
  bronchitis 26
  cough 30, 47
hormone replacement 38
hormonal changes 23
Hyssop (*Hyssopus officinalis*) 61
  bronchitis 26
  catarrh 27
  child ailment 72
  cough 30
  fever 33
  influenza 37
  insomnia 37
  poor circulation 41

illness, prevention of 9, 10 *see also* infection, resistance to
immune system strengthener 45, 58, 60
indigestion (dyspepsia) 32
  nervous 24
individual 10–11
infant 17; *see also* child, treatment of
infection, resistance to 25, 26
  strengthened 45, 58, 60
  see also illness, prevention of
inflamed surface soother 56, 63
influenza 36–7
infusion 76
insomnia 37
iron 64
itching (skin problem) 43–4
  finger/toe 27
  foot 24
  groin 24

joint inflamation (rheumatism) 42

labour, eased 41
laryngitis 37–8
Lavender (*Lavendula officinalis*) 61–2
  colic 27
  First Aid 42–52 *passim*
  headache 36
  insomnia 37
  muscle ache 39
  nervous problem 24, 40
  rheumatism 42
  whooping cough 47
Lavender, essential oil uses
  First Aid 49–52 *passim*
  headache 36
  muscle ache 39
  shingles 43
laxative 54, 57
leaf (herb) preparation 22 (table)
leg, swollen veins in 46
Lemon Balm *see* Balm
Lime Blossom (*Tilia europaea*) 62
  child ailment 72
  fever 33
  insomnia 37
  poor circulation 41
  nervous problem 24, 40
  swollen veins 27, 46
liver tonic 53, 57, 66
lung inflamation (bronchitis) 25–6

manipulation 42
Marigold (*Calendula officinalis*) 63
  athletes foot 24
  conjunctivitis 28
  mouth ulcer 39
  swollen veins 35, 46
  thrush 45
Marigold ointment 35, 46, 50
Marrubium vulgare 60–1
  bronchitis 26
  cough 30, 47

Marshmallow (*Althaea officinalis*) 63
  cough 30
  throat affection 38, 44, 45
  urinary infection 31, 46
Meadowsweet (*Filipendula ulmaria*) 11, 64
  cystitis 30
  diarrhoea 31
  indigestion 32
  morning sickness 39
  rheumatism 42
mealtime stress 32
Medicines Act (1968) 12–13, 15
medieval herbalist 9
Melissa officinalis see Balm (Lemon Balm)
menopause 38
menstruation
  cessation 38
  problems 40–1
Mentha piperita see Peppermint
Middle Ages 12
migraine 38–9; *see also* headache
morning sickness 39
mouth
  thrush infection 44–5
  ulcer 39, 59
mouthwash 39, 44
mucus, over-production 26
muscle ache/pain 39
Myrhh, Tincture of 24, 39, 44

National Health Service 15
National Institute of Medical Herbalists 10, 12, 15
natural response, illness to 10
nausea (sickness) 40
  migraine-associated 38
  pregnancy during (morning sickness) 39
  travel during 45
  see also vomiting
Nepeta cataria see Catmint
nervine 76
nervous
  exhaustion 24, 64
  problem 40
nervous system tonic 43

Nettle (*Urtica dioica*) 64
   uses 41, 43
non-addictive 15
non-toxic 11, 15
North America 9
nosebleed 51

Oats (*Avena sativa*) 64–5
   convalescence 29
   menopause 38
   nervous problem 24, 40
   shingles 43
oil, Sweet Almond 52

Peppermint (*Mentha piperita*) 65
   catarrh 27
   cold 28
   child ailment 72
   digestive disorder 32, 34
   fever 33
   headache 37
   nausea/vomiting 39, 45, 47
   period problem 41
periods
   cessation 28
   problem 40–1
piles (haemorrhoids) 34–5
poor circulation 41
   indication of 27
   strongest stimulant 55
potassium 57
poultice, hot 25
pre-menstrual tension/bloating 40–1
pregnancy 17, 41
   helpful herb 65
   herbs to avoid 59, 67
   sickness during 39
preventative medicine/measures 9, 10
psoriasis 43
puberty 23
puffiness, eyes under 26
Raspberry Leaf (*Rubus idaeus*) 65
   uses 38, 41
Red Clover (*Trifolium pratense*) 66
   bite/sting 49
   skin problem 25, 44
relaxant 53, 55, 61, 62
   definition 77
remedy, herbal *see* herbal medicines
   (remedies)
responsibility for health 10
rheumatism 42
rhinitis, allergic 35
root (herb) preparation 22 (table)
Rosemary (*Rosemarius officinalis*) 66
   convalescence 29
   flatulence 34
   headache/migraine 36, 39
   muscle ache 39
   nervous problem 40
   poor circulation 41
   shingles 43
Rosemary, essential oil uses 39, 52
Rubus idaeus 65
   uses 38, 41

Sage (*Sabria officinalis*) 66–7
   mouth ulcer 39
   throat infection 38, 44
   tonsillitis 45
salicylate 64
Sambucus nigra see Elderflower
scald (burn) 50
sciatica 42
scratch 49
sea sickness 45
sedative 37
   mild 68
self-care 12
self-healing 10, 11, 16
self-treatment, herbal medicine by 21–2
shingles 43
sickness *see* nausea; vomiting
sinusitis 43
skin problem 43–4
sleeplessness (insomnia) 37
Slippery Elm (*Ulmus fulva*) 67

boil 25
  convalescence 29
  diarrhoea 32
smelling salts 51
smoking 41
sore throat 44
'spastic colon' 68
Spirea 11
spot, inflamed 23
sprain 51–2
spring tonic 64
steam water inhalation 27
Stellaria media 56
  uses 43; of ointment 49
stimulant 55, 58, 64, 66
  definition 77
sting 49
stomach irritation, mild 53
strain 51–2
stress 24, 40
sunburn 52
survey 12, 15
Sweet Almond oil 52
swelling
  inflamed/pus-filled 23, 25
  itchy 27
Symphytum officinale see Comfrey
symptom relief 10
symptoms guide 23–52

Tanacetum parthenium 59
  migraine use 38
Taraxacum officinale 57–8
  uses 32, 42
Tea Tree, essential oil of 24, 50, 52
temperature, high 33
tension 24
throat, sore 44
thrush 44–5
Thyme (*Thymus vulgaris*) 67–8
  cough 30, 47
  digestive disorder 32, 34
  mouth ulcer 39
  throat affection 38, 44
Tilia europaea see Lime Blossom

tincture 24, 39, 44
  definition 77
toe, swelling on 27
tonic
  liver 53, 57, 66
  nervous system 43
  spring 64
  uterus 65
tonsillitis 45
tonsils, infection of 45
toxins
  excess 43
  removal 25, 54
travel expansion 9
travel sickness 45
Trifolium pratense 66
  bite/sting 49
  skin problem 25, 44
Tussilago farfora 56–7
  cough 25, 30

ulceration, stomach lining of 11
Ulmus sulva see Slippery Elm
unique, individual as 10
urinary infection 46
urination, painful 30
Urtica dioica 64
  uses 41, 43
uterus, tonic to 65

vagina, thrush infection of 44–5
Valerian (*Valeriana officinalis*) 68
  colic 27
  constipation 29
  insomnia 37
  migraine 39
  nervous problem 24, 40
  period problem 41
  sciatica 42
varicose veins 42
veins, swollen
  rectum 34–5
  legs 46

veterinary herbal medicine 73
voice loss/hoarseness 37–8
vomiting 46–7
  migraine-associated 38
  pregnancy during (morning sickness) 39
  travel during 45

warmth-inducer 60, 68
Which report (1986) 12
whole, individual as 10
'whole plants for whole people' 11
whooping cough 47
wind (flatulence) 34
Witch Hazel (*Hamamelis virginiana*) 68–9
  diarrhoea 32
  haemorrhoids 35
  cut/graze 50
women, herbs appropriate to
  Chamomile 55–6

uses 38–41 *passim*
Raspberry Leaf 65
  uses 35, 41
Oats 64–5
  uses 29, 38
  see also Balm, Ginger, Meadowsweet,
    Peppermint, Valerian
wound (cut/graze) 50, 69

Yarrow (*Achillea millefolium*) 69
  blood clotting 50, 51
  chilblains 27
  cold 28
  cystitis 30
  poor circulation 41

Zingiber officinale see Ginger